S0-ARL-250

JAMES
How Faith Works

The wisdom that comes from heaven is first of all pure; then peace-loving, considerate, submissive, full of mercy and good fruit, impartial and sincere. Peacemakers who sow in peace raise a harvest of righteousness.

James 3:17

Compiled by Lorraine Groth

CONCORDIA PUBLISHING HOUSE • SAINT LOUIS

Copyright © 1995 Concordia Publishing House
3558 South Jefferson Avenue, St. Louis, MO 63118-3968
Manufactured in the United States of America

Series editors: Thomas J. Doyle and Rodney L. Rathmann

Scripture taken from the HOLY BIBLE, NEW INTERNATIONAL VERSION®. NIV®. Copyright © 1973, 1978, 1984 by International Bible Society. Used by permission of Zondervan Publishing House. All rights reserved.

We solicit your comments and suggestions concerning this material. Please write to Product Manager, Adult Bible Studies, Concordia Publishing House, 3558 S. Jefferson Avenue, St. Louis, MO 63118-3968.

All rights reserved. No part of this publication may be reproduced, stored in a retrieval system, or transmitted, in any form or by any means, electronic, mechanical, photocopying, recording, or otherwise, without the prior written permission of Concordia Publishing House.

7   8   9   10   11   12   13   14   10   09   08   07   06   05   04

Contents

Lesson 1

A Greeting to Some Special Slaves (James 1:1)

Theme Verse

"James, a servant of God and of the Lord Jesus Christ" **(James 1:1).**

Goal

In this lesson we will look at who wrote the letter of James, to whom it was written, and the occasion for the letter. We will also discover how James continues to speak to us today.

What's Going On Here?

Apart from the opening greeting **(1:1)**, James' letter is more of a sermon in style than a letter. In five short chapters James offers pastoral encouragement and rebuke to his people both in Palestine and scattered abroad. Since James is addressing those who already believe in Christ as Savior, he does not attempt to systematically outline the basics of the Christian faith for them (justification). Rather, his purpose is to encourage his readers to live the faith they profess to believe (sanctification). James repeatedly points out that genuine faith in Christ will always evidence itself in the believer's life through fruits of faith—Christlike living and loving. After spelling out the practical implications faith in Christ has for their lives, he challenges them to put these into action.

Searching the Scriptures

About the Greeting

1. In the Greek, the original language of this letter, the word translated

by the English word "servant" means slave. Why do you think James used the word "slave"?

2. How does our attitude toward God—our "picture" of Him (Father, Judge, King, Friend)—affect the way we understand the word "slave" or servant?

3. As you read **verse 1** and glance through the entire letter, do the spirit and tone of James as well as his words suggest (1) an angry slave relationship, or (2) a joyful servant relationship? Why?

4. What words in **verse 1** set this letter apart as a Christian epistle? What words, beside "servant," are a Christian's confession of faith? To help you answer this question, look up **Matthew 16:16; John 6:68–69;** and **1 Corinthians 12:3**.

To Whom Was James Written?

1. Do you think that the letter was addressed to Jews, to Christians, or to Christians who for the most part were formerly Jews (like the disciples themselves)? Check on the meaning of "twelve tribes" **(Genesis 49:28)** and "dispersion" (see **1 Peter 1:1, 17; Hebrews 11:13–16**).

2. What indicates that the letter is addressed also to you?

Is It Really a Letter?

1. One of the interesting points about the epistle of James is that it does not have all the characteristics that we ordinarily associate with a letter. In the first verse, what is the only real indication that the writing of James is a letter?

2. Compare **James** with **3 John**. What characteristics of a letter do you find in **3 John** but not in **James?**

3. James uses imperatives often. He gives commands and directives. Imperatives occur most often in sermons or instructions. Examples in James' letter are "take note of this" **(1:19)** and "listen" **(2:5)**. (In this short letter, James uses imperatives 54 times. What others can you find?) Because of the frequent use of the imperative, many say that James only appears to be a letter; it really is a work designed to teach and to encourage. Do you agree? Why or why not?

Who Really Wrote James?

1. The author of the book identifies himself as James **(1:1).** But who was James? Check a Bible dictionary. How many do you find? Who were they?

2. Of the different men called James in the New Testament, James the Lord's brother **(Matthew 13:55–56)**, who is said to have been martyred in the mid-60s, is the only one given consistent serious consideration as a possible author. During Jesus' lifetime James did not believe in Him as Savior **(John 7:5)**. What evidently happened to James after the risen Jesus made an appearance to him **(1 Corinthians 15:7; Acts 1:14)**?

3. What do the following passages say about James, the Lord's brother: **Acts 15:4, 13–19; 21:17–18; Galatians 1:18–19?** How does Paul refer to him in **Galatians 2:9?**

4. Students of Scripture marvel at James' simple yet authoritative self-identification in the opening address. They say that only James the brother of the Lord and respected leader of the church at Jerusalem could characteristically and authentically have identified himself in this way. What do you think?

The Word for Us

1. Read **Romans 1:9; 2 Timothy 1:3;** and **1 Peter 2:16.** Discuss what it means to you to be a "slave" of God through Jesus Christ.

2. Does our place as slaves make our choices harder or easier? Think of a recent decision you made about something significant in your life. How did your faith in Christ contribute to your decision-making process? Did it help to make the process easier or more difficult?

3. Are we expected to "work" for something as slaves?

4. What difference does our place as slaves make in our relationships with each other? Think of two or three people in your circle of friends and co-workers whom you could serve in a concrete way. List what you want to do for them (i.e., send someone an encouraging note, mow a widow's lawn).

5. In what sense are we freer as slaves of God than we would be as slaves of ourselves?

Closing

Pray the following prayer.

Dear Lord, we give You thanks for today, especially for the opportunity to come together to study Your Word and for the enabling power of the Holy Spirit to put what we learn into practice. Help us this week and in the weeks to come as we study the book of James to apply Your Word to our lives so that we may be conformed to the image of Christ and live our faith in both word and deed. In Jesus' name we ask this. Amen.

Lesson 2

Joy in the Midst of Joylessness (James 1:2–8)

Theme Verse

"Consider it pure joy, my brothers, whenever you face trials of many kinds, because you know that the testing of your faith develops perseverance" **(James 1:2–3)**.

Goal

In this lesson we will gain a new appreciation for how God uses trials to help us grow and mature in our Christian faith.

What's Going On Here?

In this first part of his letter, James encourages his fellow believers to have joy in the face of trials. Note that James doesn't say *if* but *whenever* they face trials. He knows that they are experiencing hardships that test their faith—and will likely experience more—but that it is possible for them to profit from these testings. James encourages his readers to ask God for wisdom and strength and allow Him to use their hardships to develop in them patience and Christian maturity. Through these trials God is molding them into the image of His Suffering Servant, Jesus. This is a cause for real joy!

Searching the Scriptures

Why Joy Is Real

1. How do the following words and phrases draw attention to the underlying unity of Christian thought in James' epistle?

Verse 1: "a servant of God and of the Lord Jesus Christ, To the twelve tribes scattered among the nations"

2: "my brothers"

3: "the testing of your faith"

4: "complete, not lacking anything"

5: "ask God, who gives generously to all without finding fault, and it will be given to him"

6: "when he asks, he must believe"

2. James says to "consider it pure joy … whenever you face trials." Give an example of how a Christian may have joy even while experiencing a trial.

Are You As Lonely As You Feel?

1. What does the word "trial" mean as James uses it in **verse 2?** Why does a person tend to feel more lonely when he or she undergoes a "trial"?

2. What is there in **verse 1** to indicate that a Christian never really stands alone? Why is it important for a person experiencing a trial to trust in God's Word, rather than in his or her own feelings?

3. How does remembering the promise of **Romans 8:28** help us to face trials with joy?

Why Tests?

1. Every youngster in school asks, "Why tests?" Why does God give us tests? What does James say about that in **verse 3?**

2. James teaches that it is God's purpose to develop Christians who are mature and complete. Can you think of a trial or hardship in your life that God used to help you grow in Christ? What did you learn? How did this help your faith grow?

3. What insight—and reassurance—do the following Bible passages give you: **Romans 5:1–6; 1 Peter 1:3–7; Hebrews 12:7–11?** What words of Scripture have helped you when you have been down and out?

Faith in Christ, Not Moralism

1. Patience and steadfastness are often considered characteristics of a person of good moral character. In what way is James presenting patience as something more than a virtue or moral ideal?

2. Is faith a virtue, part of a moral ideal we strive to achieve, or is it more? Give an example of how you live out your faith in Christ in a practical way in your daily life. How can we help others keep faith as a practical reality in their lives?

Pray for Wisdom

1. List some meanings for the word *wisdom*. What does James mean by the word in **verse 5**? What other words with basically the same meaning from **verses 3–4** could be used in **verse 5** for "wisdom"? See also **Romans 8:26–27.**

2. In **verse 5,** James writes that anyone lacking wisdom should ask God for it. What does it mean when we ask God that we "must believe and not doubt" **(v. 6)**? Is there a difference between merely asking God and asking Him in faith? Explain.

3. In what way is "having a question" different from "doubting"? May they ever be the same? How are "doubt" and "trust" opposites? How is wavering between doubt and trust (being "double-minded," **v. 8**) a "trial" in itself? What does it mean when James says that one who doubts is like a wave of the sea that is tossed by the wind **(v. 6)?**

4. How does James describe the doubter in **verses 7** and **8?** Do you see yourself there? What is the remedy for our doubt?

5. How does the Holy Spirit keep a believer from wandering back and forth from this opinion to that **(v. 6)?** How does the Holy Spirit lead us to find fulfillment and completion in our Lord Jesus Christ? Use **John 14:27** and **Philippians 4:7** to help you.

The Word for Us

1. Have you ever had doubts? Have you ever been double-minded? How did other Christians help you? How can James be of help to you in such times?

2. How do you help people who doubt and are double-minded when they face trials?

3. How do James' words in this section work out in daily life? Do the following exercise. Take any problem you have—one that is a trial for you, not just a passing thought.

a. Write down several possibilities for what God may be trying to teach you through this verse.

b. What does it mean to you, as you consider your problem, that Jesus Christ died for the guilt and punishment of your sins, and rose again in victory over all the powers of evil and death?

c. Since in Holy Baptism God gave you the promise of forgiveness and inheritance in His everlasting kingdom, what assurance do you have that God will give you protection and care now, even though your life continues to have trials and problems? Ask God for the ability to respond to this problem with renewed faith in Him and trust that He will bring good out of this trial for you.

d. Responding to trials can be difficult when you feel you are alone. Who are some people you could ask to regularly meet with you to help encourage and pray for you?

e. What encouragement can you offer to someone else suffering trials?

Closing

Pray the following prayer together.

Heavenly Father, help us to remember when trials and testings come our way that You have promised to bring good out of all things—even these—for us. Use these hardships to help us mature in our faith in Christ. Strengthen us when our faith and trust grow weak, and by Your Spirit enable us to turn to You for wisdom and guidance. Finally, use us, Father, as sources of comfort and encouragement to other Christians when they too experience trials, reminding them of Your love, Your presence, and Your purpose. We ask this in Jesus' name. Amen.

Lesson 3

Don't Blame God
(James 1:9–15)

Theme Verse

"Blessed is the man who perseveres under trial, because when he has stood the test, he will receive the crown of life" **(James 1:12).**

Goal

Our purpose in this lesson is twofold: (1) to appreciate that our status before God is not dependent on our wealth or position in this world but solely on Christ, who died for us; and (2) to rejoice in knowing that, after we have endured the trials of this life, by God's grace we will receive the "crown of life"—eternal life with Him.

What's Going On Here?

James' discussion of the poor and rich man appears between two sections on trials. Perhaps he placed it here to connect wealth and poverty with trials and testings. The Christian can rejoice in knowing he is rich because of his faith in Christ. James notes that worldly wealth means nothing to God. It is what is in the heart that is of eternal significance to Him. Thus, Christians find true wealth by developing their spiritual lives, not their bank accounts. By remaining faithful to God, with the Spirit's help, throughout the storms of life, they receive the crown of life. This victory crown is not fame, power, wealth, or prestige here on earth, but eternal life with God forever.

In **verses 13–15** James points out that we are prone to blame others, even God, for our problems. While God allows temptations to come our way in order to refine our faith, He does not tempt anyone to sin. We need to recognize that it is our own evil desires and sin that pull us down, and that we need to confess our wrongdoing and to receive forgiveness in Christ.

Searching the Scriptures

Just Who Are the Humble and the Rich?

1. It is easy to become confused about what it means to be humble and rich before God. The word "humble" in **verse 9** has various meanings. In contrast to the word "rich" in **verse 10,** what picture do you have of humble circumstances?

2. In view of the entire verse, the word "humble" may refer as well to one who is beat down and overwhelmed by trials **(vv. 2–3).** It may also refer to the person who repents of his or her sinfulness. How are these last two meanings related?

3. In what "high position" can a person in humble circumstances rejoice **(v. 9)?**

4. Why is the rich person to "boast" in his humiliation but not in his riches? Read **Psalm 103:15–16** and explain what the words of the psalm and of **verses 10–11** mean to you. To the rich man?

5. What may the Christian boast of? Is boasting ever really good?

Does It Make a Difference?

1. How are you both "poor" and "rich" in your life?

2. Put **verses 9–11** in your own words.

3. As a Christian, how does the Word of God speak to you in order to help you remain faithful to God in both good and bad times? See **2 Timothy 3:14–17.**

4. Why is it sometimes harder to be faithful when we are wealthy and full of the goodness of life?

Getting Crowned

1. James' statement in **verse 12** seems to indicate that blessing comes as a result of our ability to endure "trials." Is perseverance or endurance itself a cause of blessing? What or who enables a Christian to persevere under trials? What relationship is there between perseverance and fruit of faith **(Galatians 5:22–26)?**

2. What does James mean by the phrase "crown of life"?

Does God Tempt Us?

1. What is the difference between a trial and a temptation? Is every trial necessarily a temptation?

2. Although God allows trials **(v. 2; Hebrews 12:7–11)**, James emphatically says that "God cannot be tempted by evil, nor does He tempt anyone" **(1:13)**. Why is the fact that God does not tempt us to do wrong so important? Use the following Bible passages to help you answer the question: **2 Timothy 1:9–10; Titus 1:2; Leviticus 19:2; Romans 1:17.**

3. It is not God but evil (our own sinfulness, Satan) that tempts us. We are tempted to give up God's gift of salvation when we are seduced (enticed, **v. 14**) to take "other gifts"—things that in our sinfulness seem to be strikingly desirable.

a. Whom do we usually blame for our sins? Why are we so hesitant to blame ourselves? Whom did Adam and Eve blame **(Genesis 3:11–13)**?

b. With the freedom to keep your answers to yourselves and God, what are your inner personal temptations?

c. What are some temptations from the evil in the world that tug at you?

d. What are some past personal trials and temptations that through His Word God has enabled you to remain faithful to Him so that by His grace you remained patient and steadfast and ended up not really lacking in anything (vv. 3–4)?

e. What are some trials and temptations confronting you now, for which you trust God to lead you through and to help you overcome?

Give "Birth" to Death?

1. It is interesting to note the imagery of conception, birth, and death that James uses in **verses 14–15.** Note the ironic contrast. Usually conception and birth bring forth life. That was God's purpose at the creation in the beginning. It is also God's purpose for the new creation through Jesus Christ. Explain in your own words what James states by means of the birth imagery of **verse 15?**

2. To change imagery a bit, in what way is sin like corruption? If you left a rotten apple in a carton with other apples, what eventually would happen? With what imagery does Paul in the first seven words of **Romans 6:23** say the same thing as James in **verse 15?** Is the effect of the ironic contrast between "full-grown" and "death" (**v. 15**) Law or Gospel?

3. No wonder James emphasizes that God does not tempt us! God is gracious, good, life-giving. Evil destroys, not God. He creates and redeems. The crown of life is a gift that God offers to us for Christ's sake. Trusting Him for it, we shall receive it. That is God's promise. Reread **verse 12.**

The Word for Us

1. God does not tempt us, but He does allow tests to our faith. What is the difference between testing and tempting?

2. If God really loves us, why doesn't He protect us from all temptations?

3. Think of some personal trials you are facing right now. What can the church do to support you and help you persevere (e.g., offer a prayer group, offer financial planning advice, provide marital or family counseling, etc.)?

4. Why is it reassuring to know the crown of life is a gift of God's grace, not something we earn?

Closing

Pray together stanza 5 of " 'Come, Follow Me,' Said Christ, the Lord."

Then let us follow Christ, our Lord,
And take the cross appointed
And, firmly clinging to His word,
In suff'ring be undaunted.
For those who bear the battle's strain
The crown of heav'nly life obtain.

Lesson 4

True Religion
(James 1:16–27)

Theme Verse

"Do not merely listen to the word … . Do what it says" **(James 1:22)**.

Goal

That we might better understand that it is the Gospel of Jesus Christ that gives us freedom from sin and freedom to serve God faithfully—to become "doers" of the Word.

What's Going On Here?

James underscores in **verse 17** that not only does God not tempt anyone to sin but He is, indeed, the Source of every good thing. God always wills what is best for His children and gives us what we need for His purposes to be carried out. The best gift He gives us is new birth in Christ. This new birth is accomplished when God brings us to faith in Christ through the Gospel—His Word of truth.

Finally, James underscores in **verses 19–27** how the new life in Christ will evidence itself in our lives: eager to please the Lord who died for us, we find happiness in being doers of His Word—by using godly speech, by living a righteous life, and by compassionately caring for the needs of others.

Searching the Scriptures
Temptations Offer Only the Best

1. Have any of your temptations ever offered you anything less than the

"true," the "pure," the "best"? What was the "good" offer that Satan made to Adam and Eve **(Genesis 3:4–5)?** How might Adam and Eve have justified their choice?

2. What "true" and "pure" gifts did Satan offer Jesus in the wilderness **(Luke 4:1–13)?**

3. In contrast to Adam and Eve, how did Jesus (the second Adam, **1 Corinthians 15:45**) overcome temptation? In whom did Jesus trust? In whose Word did Jesus trust?

4. How do your answers to the last two questions work for you also during times of temptation? Think of your recent experiences of temptation. How did the person Jesus Christ "keep the faith" for us?

"I Believe ..."

1. **Verses 17–18** are a proclamation of the goodness of God—a type of creedal statement. What features of the Christian faith do you see in the verses? What, for instance, is the significance of the name "Father" **(v. 17)?** Does it have the same significance in the Apostles' Creed? (See **Matthew 7:11.**)

2. In **verse 17,** what is the meaning of the phrase "Father of the heavenly lights"? Today people seem to seek guidance from other lights—the stars, through astrology. What does James' statement here say to them? Compare **Genesis 1:3–5** and **14–19.**

3. Since God does not change in any way (like shifting shadows, **v. 17**), what assurance does that give us when weakness or difficulty tempt us to think God is unjust or unfair to us **(v. 13)?**

4. In what way do **verses 4** and **12** affirm the statement of **verse 17?**

Born to Live

1. Compare and contrast the imagery in **verses 15** and **18.** How is our new birth God's doing, not ours? (See **John 1:12–13; 3:5; Titus 3:5**).

2. What does the word "firstfruits" **(v. 18)** mean? How are Christians firstfruits of Christ's death and resurrection? In what way is your life a "firstfruits" of God's work in you?

3. Even though the Holy Spirit is not mentioned in **verse 18** (nor in the entire epistle), what evidence of the work of the Holy Spirit do you find?

Listening and Doing

1. Too often we talk more than we listen. James advises us to do just the opposite: "Everyone should be quick to listen, slow to speak" **(v. 19).** Why is this good advice?

2. In **verse 19** James is not referring to righteous anger over immoral injustices, but to sinful anger that erupts when our feelings get hurt. Whenever we are angry, we are quick to blame someone else. Why do we often want to blame even God? Why is it so hard to listen when we are angry?

3. What is the connection between "man's anger" **(v. 20)** and "moral filth and the evil that is so prevalent" **(v. 21)**? Relate your answer to **verse 15**. In view of your answer how does anger keep us from listening to God and doing what He wants, thus blocking His work and Word?

4. How does sinful anger give a negative witness to the Gospel?

"In One Ear and ..." Why Not?

1. In **verse 22** James refers to another way of deceiving oneself. What is it? What is the effect of listening to the Word in church or reading the Bible, but never doing as it says?

2. Why is it impossible for the person who believes in Christ as Savior to be only a hearer and not a doer?

3. What does James mean when he writes that a person who is a hearer only is like a person who observes himself in a mirror and then forgets what he is like **(vv. 23–24)?**

4. James says the doer will be "blessed in what he does" **(v. 25).** In contrast to the unbeliever, who is a slave to sin, the Christian has the joyous freedom to be what God created him to be. What do the following phrases say about the blessings that comes from being a doer of the Word?

Verse 3: testing of your faith produces steadfastness, or patience

4: perfect and complete, lacking in nothing

12: he will receive the crown of life

Motivated by the Gospel

1. If taken out of context, the first half of **verse 25** may be difficult. One might be tempted to think that the phrase "perfect law that gives freedom" refers to the Law of God rather than to the Gospel. Actually, it refers to the entire Word of God. But in this verse the emphasis is particularly on the Gospel of forgiveness. It is the Gospel of Jesus Christ which gives us freedom from sin and the freedom to serve God fruitfully in faith to Him. How can we be sure of that? Read **Galatians 3.** Compare **verse 18** and the last half of **verse 21.**

2. **James 1:26–27** gives a good detailed statement and example of what it means to be a doer of God's Word—one who acts. How do **verses 19–20** help you to explain **verse 26?** How do **verses 23–24** serve as a contrast to **verse 27?**

3. **Verse 27** sums it up—and probably better than we realize at first reading. Here holiness and pureness inevitably go together, for example, when visiting orphans and widows in their affliction. Why are we not skeptical when James talks about "pure" and "faultless" religion?

The Word for Us

1. Why is it not possible to live a holy life in isolation from other people?

2. How does a concern for getting rid of "moral filth" relate to political and social action? What are some current areas where a Christian might take a stand?

3. In what way does **verse 27** describe you and the ministry of your congregation? What are some practical ways that you and your church can care for widows and orphans and others who need a Christian advocate? Do you see any need for repentance and improvement?

Closing

Pray together stanzas 1, 3, and 5 of "O God of Mercy, God of Light."

O God of mercy, God of light,
In love and mercy infinite,
Teach us, as ever in Your sight,
To live our lives in You.

Teach us the lesson Jesus taught:
To feel for those His blood has bought,
That ev'ry deed and word and thought
May work a work for You.

In sickness, sorrow, want, or care,
Each other's burdens help us share;
May we, where help is needed, there
Give help as though to You.

Lesson 5

From Partiality
to Servanthood
(James 2:1–13)

Theme Verse

"Love your neighbor as yourself" **(James 2:8).**

Goal

That we may look at others the way God does in Jesus Christ, not valuing them for what they have, but who they are—God's redeemed children, rich in faith.

What's Going On Here?

In this section James argues against favoritism. He says that any time we value other people for what they have or do, rather than for who they are, we show partiality.

In keeping with Old and New Testament teaching, James notes that God looks at a person's heart rather than assets. He is a compassionate God who has "chosen those who are poor in the eyes of the world to be rich in faith" **(v. 5).** As in Jesus' Sermon on the Mount **(Matthew 5:3),** "poor" here refers to those who are spiritually poor. Believers do not deserve God's grace. Yet, He has chosen them to inherit His Kingdom. Since all Christians have received this undeserved mercy from God, they should express this same Christlike mercy and love towards others without showing partiality.

Searching the Scriptures

Partial! Who, Me?

1. Partiality (favoring one person or group above another for superficial reasons) is prejudice. The people at the time of the New Testament were affected by appearances **(2:1)** and made judgments on externals. Do we?

2. List partialities that tempt you: What people do you tend to overlook in a gathering, or "not see" when you walk by, or dismiss from your mind when hearing about them? Does your community show partiality? your congregation? your school?

3. Why do faith in Jesus Christ and partiality not go together **(2:1)**? Is God partial? How do you explain that although God judges and discriminates against all evil in the world and the sinfulness in our lives, yet He is not partial?

4. James says that whenever we are judgmental and show partiality we set ourselves up in the place of God as judges **(2:4–5)**. As self-styled judges, do we use ourselves or God's Word as a standard for our judgment?

5. Why does James say that in being partial we become judges "with evil thoughts" **(2:4)?** In saying that, is James himself being judgmental, or is he expressing a proper judgment?

There's Always a Reason

1. Read **James 2:2–4.** There are many reasons why people show partiality. Can you list some?

2. What connection is there between partiality and double-mindedness? Why will a double-minded person change in his partiality from one person and point of view to another? How do James' words in **1:7–8** apply to such a person?

3. Why do you suppose that in this section about not showing partiality **(2:1–13)**, James twice appeals to his readers as "brothers" **(2:1, 5)?**

Rich in Faith

1. Why are poor people easy victims? How are the poor discriminated against? Can you give examples from your own life? On the other hand, have you ever taken advantage of the poor?

2. James says that the poor in the eyes of the world are "rich in faith" (2:5). Are the Christian-poor heirs of the Kingdom because they are economically poor? Why or why not? Compare **Matthew 5:3**. What is it that gives eternal life to the poor (1:21)?

Here Comes the Judge

1. Read **James 2:6.** Does James mean that the rich are always oppressors? Why is the temptation to oppress more real for the rich? Why is it more likely that the rich "drag" the poor to court than vice versa?

2. Is a legal decision always morally right? How can you tell the difference between what is moral and what is legal? How does James' question in **2:4** help you? Discuss other examples of how government, law, and the courts are used wrongly. What is your civic responsibility as a Christian?

The Sting of the Law

1. In **2:9** James says partiality is always sinful. Relate James' statement in **2:9** to **1:14.**

2. If "love" is the fulfilling of the Law (v. 8), then the misuse of persons is breaking the Law. How is partiality related to the commandments? Give examples.

3. Why is a person who breaks just one law guilty of breaking all of them? What does 2:10–11 have to say to us if we think that God might be kind to us and save us because we keep most of the Law?

The Servanthood of Royalty

1. In **verse 8** what is the "royal law"? What is there in **2:8** to suggest that James does not expect anyone really to have fulfilled the royal law? What connection is there between the "royal law" and "the law that gives freedom" (2:12)?

2. Can the Ten Commandments motivate us to love God, and our neighbor as ourselves? How do the following verses help you to answer those questions: 1:1, 5, 12, 18 and 2:1, 5? What only enables us to "speak and act as those who are going to be judged by the law that gives freedom" (2:12)?

3. How does mercy triumph over judgment **(2:13)?** How does **2:5** help you to answer that question?

4. Does the phrase "mercy triumphs over judgment" characterize our society? Does it characterize you?

The Word for Us

1. Can riches ever be a sign of God's favor? What is a God-pleasing attitude towards our material wealth?

2. Evaluate your prayer life. How often do you pray for material blessings over other concerns? How do we keep our materialistic spirit in check?

3. Look at your daily newspaper and mark examples of partiality, discrimination, and prejudice. In private confession to God, would you have to admit seeing your name in place of the names that you see in the newspaper? Do you find at times that the system, or "the way we are" in society and the world in our patterns of living, has a "built-in" prejudice? Give an example.

4. Should we just go along with the way things are at work or in school or in our community—even though we know they are wrong—or should we try to change them?

Closing

Speak together stanzas 4 and 5 of "O Fount of Good, for All Your Love" as a closing prayer.

Then help us, Lord, Your yoke to wear
And joyful do Your will,
Each other's burdens gladly share,
The law of love fulfill.

Your face with rev'rence and with love
We in Your poor would view,
And while we minister to them
Would do it as to You.

Lesson 6

The Fruitfulness of Faith in Christ (James 2:14–26)

Theme Verse

"Faith by itself, if it is not accompanied by action, is dead" (**James 2:17**).

Goal

That we might better understand the relationship between faith and works and strive by the power of the Holy Spirit to put our faith into action in word and deed.

What's Going On Here?

The relationship between faith and works is as important a theological topic today as it was during the Reformation. The Reformers maintained that we are saved by faith in Christ alone (*sola fide*), not by works or by faith as a work. They based this on the clear witness of such Bible passages as **Romans 3:28; Ephesians 2:8–9;** and **Galatians 2:15–16.** The Reformers were also quick to point out, however, that saving faith always results in works done out of faith.

In this section of his epistle, James is not contradicting that we are saved by faith alone. Rather he is challenging his readers and all those who confess faith in Christ to put faith into action. He underscores that genuine faith will always produce thoughts, words, and deeds that reflect the Savior. As a result, anyone who "*claims*" to have faith but has no deeds ought to check his spiritual pulse to see if his faith is still alive.

Searching the Scriptures

Is Dead Faith Still "Faith"?

1. What does James mean by the word "faith" **(2:14)?** In whom does this faith center?

2. How is James' question in **2:14** a summary of what he has been saying all along about impatience, double-mindedness, and partiality?

3. James flatly states that faith that does not act is dead **(2:17).** Can faith and works ever be separated? Why or why not? What value are "works" without faith in Christ? What value is "faith" without its fruits, or the works of faith?

4. Is it true that faith is invisible without works? What word does James use to describe faith without works **(2:17)?**

5. The example in **2:15–16** needs special attention. One of the criticisms against Christian people and against the church is that individual Christians and organizations of Christians talk concern for others but do not always act to help. (Note the parallel between **1:22–25** and **2:14–18**.) Have you ever heard that criticism being made? Have you ever made it yourself? Has the criticism ever been made about you? What are some practical steps you or your church can take to build a new image?

Actions Speak Louder Than Words

1. Consider the hurt and the cause for complaint in the following:

a. My husband or wife says he/she loves me, but seldom talks to me.

b. The church talks about the Gospel and about love, but doesn't want to get involved in the problems of the community.

c. People who are well dressed and have big homes receive a more hearty welcome at the church door than the poor people.

What examples from the epistle of James and other parts of Scripture can you add to the above list?

2. What examples can you give from your own life experiences?

Head Knowledge Only

1. What is "head knowledge"? Why can one say that faith in Christ without the fruits of faith is head knowledge only? Relate your answer to what James says about the devils in **2:19.** What do you have that the devils don't

have? Why do the devils shudder?

2. Compare **James 2:14–18** to **Matthew 7:16–20** and **Luke 6:43–44.** How is James amplifying Jesus' teaching?

3. James seems to be giving a choice between faith and works in **2:18.** How does **Galatians 5:6** help you understand the relationship of faith and works?

Are You a Classic Example?

1. Abraham and Rahab **(vv. 21** and **25)** are classic examples, especially to the Jewish Christians who knew their Scripture (Old Testament). Abraham is called the patriarch of the chosen people of Israel. What promises did God make to Abraham and to his descendants **(Genesis 12:1–3; 15:1–6; 17:1–8)?**

2. Did Abraham believe God's promise to him? See especially **Genesis 15:6.** How did Abraham's faith in God show itself in obedience (fruits of faith, good works)? What magnificent act of faith was Abraham asked to do? Was he willing? (See **Genesis 22:1–19** and **Hebrews 11:17.**)

3. Compare **2:21–24** with **Galatians 3:6–9.** (See also **Hebrews 11:8–12.**) Is there a contradiction? What does the context tell you? How does the fact that Paul was writing to those who thought they could be made right with God by keeping the letter of the Law and that James wrote to those who wanted to be Christians in name and "do their own thing" help you to understand the difference?

4. Rahab **(2:25)** is another classic example of faith in God. Read **Joshua 2:4, 15; 6:17.** How did she demonstrate her faith? How does she demonstrate James' statement in **2:22?**

The Word for Us

1. Read all of **Hebrews 11.** How was the faith of each person shown? For example, how did Noah **(Hebrews 11:7; Genesis 6–8)** and Moses **(Hebrews 11:23–27; Exodus 2–3)** illustrate James' statement that "his faith and his actions were working together, and his faith was made complete by what he did" **(2:22)?**

2. How does the account of David **(Hebrews 11:32)** fighting Goliath **(1 Samuel 17)** make the same point? Do you find any contradiction between your answers and the biblical principle of grace alone and faith alone? Do you find any contradiction with what Paul wrote in **Ephesians 2:8–9?**

3. Reflect on this past week, remembering that you are saved by grace through faith and not by what you did or did not do. Then think of specific examples of how your faith made a difference in what you did. Share some of these.

Closing

Close with silent prayer, asking God for forgiveness when your faith did not seem to make a difference this past week as well as the strengthening power of the Holy Spirit to do better. Praise God for the evidence of faith you did see.

Lesson 7

A Treacherous Tongue
(James 3:1–12)

Theme Verse

"Out of the same mouth come praise and cursing. My brothers, this should not be" **(James 3:10).**

Goal

That we might take seriously the harm our tongues cause, receive the assurance of Christ's forgiveness for this, and learn to use our tongues wisely with the Spirit's power, governed by the question, "What would Jesus say and do?"

What's Going On Here?

James continues his emphasis on a living faith by focusing on how our tongues get us into trouble. He scathingly comments that the tongue corrupts the whole person, cannot be tamed, and is a restless evil. "Out of the same mouth come praise and cursing. My brothers, this should not be" **(3:10)** he exclaims.

The Christian's problem with his tongue stems from a heart problem caused by the old sinful nature. In a series of pictures James goes on to emphasize that God has given us new hearts in Christ, and because of this, we will bear Christlike fruit. Apart from Christ, no one can control his tongue, but with a new heart, guided by the Holy Spirit, we can turn from our old ways and find new strength to use our tongues to glorify God and build up those around us.

Searching the Scriptures

For the Teacher

1. Why would James choose this place in his letter for his counsel to those who might want to be teachers? What connection is there between James' statement about teachers and the material in the previous verses (**2:18–24**) about the fruits of faith in God? In what way does James' advice to teachers serve as an introduction to what he writes later about the tongue?

2. Why does James say "we who teach will be judged more strictly" (**3:1**)? Is that fair? Who will be the judge?

3. James says that we all make mistakes (**3:2**), not just teachers. If a person made no mistakes in what he said, what would he be like (**3:2**)? Do you know of any one like that (**2 Corinthians 5:21**)? Why do you suppose that instead of writing "we all make a few mistakes" James writes that we "stumble in many ways" (**3:2**)?

Imagery: The Language of Pictures

1. The successive images that James uses in **3:3–5** are quite expressive. What is a "bit" (**3:3**)? If you have driven a team of horses, or ridden a pony, you know that it takes only a slight tug on the rein to guide the horses. How does that "light touch" add to the meaning of **3:3**?

2. What further examples can you give of small things controlled by big things? And which is the most deadly of "little" things (3:5)?

The Terrible Tongue

1. "The tongue is a small part of the body, but it makes great boasts" (3:5). The tongue has power. Its activity affects our whole life. Just how powerful is it according to 3:5? How is the tongue like a spark?

2. Why is the boasting of the tongue out of place? See **Genesis 8:21b; Galatians 5:19; James 2:4.**

Hell's Representative

1. James expands on the evil nature of the tongue. He calls it "a world of evil" among the parts of the body. What does he mean by this?

2. What connection is there between the "world of evil" of the tongue (3:6) and what James writes in 1:14–15, 19–20, or in 2:14–17?

3. How does the tongue corrupt the whole person **(3:6)?** How does your explanation relate to what Paul wrote in **Romans 8:18–23?**

4. Explain what James means when he writes that the tongue is "set on fire by hell" **(3:6).** How do you relate that to **John 8:44?**

Wanted: A Tongue Tamer

1. **Verse 8** indicates that our struggle to tame our tongue is doomed. Why? What is the "deadly poison"?

2. Who can tame the tongue? Why does this portion of Scripture make us focus again on the forgiveness of God in Jesus Christ?

A Paradox

1. Read **verses 9–12.** What is the answer to the question in these verses? Does the fact that fig trees cannot produce olives mean that sinners cannot do good?

2. James seems to imply that if our tongue does evil we are altogether evil. In what sense is that true? What tree do we have **(1 Peter 2:24)** that permits us to bear good fruit?

3. Since we are constantly led astray by our tongue, we should daily repent. Where does our comfort lie? See **1 John 1:9.**

The Word for Us

1. What kind of damage does a tongue used in a destructive way do to various relationships (e.g., one's marriage, at church)?

2. Discuss specific problems Christians may have with the use of their tongues (for instance, lying, gossiping, bragging, controlling, belittling others). Think about which ones cause you the most trouble.

3. How can other Christians help you in your struggle to use your tongue in a God-pleasing way? (For example, pray for you, form a support group where members provide accountability, memorize Scripture with you, etc.) Think of one or two people whom you will ask for help with a specific tongue problem.

4. List ways you can use your tongue in a positive way, e.g., to encourage, pray, compliment, pray, give gentle answers, speak out for those in need of an advocate. Choose one of these and make a game plan for how you will implement it this week. For example, if you wish to pray, list the people and concerns you want to address in your prayer time.

Closing

Close by praying stanzas 1 and 3 of "Take My Life, O Lord, Renew."

Take my life, O Lord, renew,
Consecrate my heart to You;
Take my moments and my days;
Let them sing your ceaseless praise.

Take my voice and let me sing
Praises to my Savior King;
Take my lips and keep them true,
Filled with messages from You.

Lesson 8

The Wisdom of Faith
(James 3:13–18)

Theme Verse

"The wisdom that comes from heaven is ... pure; then peace-loving, considerate, submissive, full of mercy and good fruit" **(James 3:17)**.

Goal

In this lesson we seek to understand the difference between God's wisdom and the world's wisdom so that we may by the power of the Holy Spirit make wise choices and have lives that reflect our faith in Christ.

What's Going On Here?

In these passages James contrasts the world's wisdom to true wisdom. The world's wisdom is alluring. It promises power, prestige, and wealth to those who selfishly look out for number one first and ambitiously strive to get ahead. Godly wisdom, on the other hand, is not just acquired information applied to a given situation for earthly gain. Rather, it combines practical skills in living with spiritual insights. It seeks to follow God's design and makes choices based on His Word rather than the world's standards.

In **verse 13** James notes that wisdom like faith will show itself in works. He spells out what a person of godly wisdom will be like: He or she will not be envious, selfish, ambitious, or boastful. Rather, acting in a manner that is consistent with the new nature in Christ, he or she will be peace-loving, considerate, submissive, full of mercy, and good fruit.

Searching the Scriptures
The Unwisdom of the Wise

1. We are very flattered when people mark us as wise and understanding. But we have to confess that we are not consistent in using the understanding and wisdom we do have. Our sinful self is always at war with the new person we are in Christ. Our tongue (**3:9**) exposes us. It reveals the battle. We have not yet obtained perfection. At times, our thoughts and actions may show considerable understanding. Our emotions in control, we act in a reasonably constant way. Then, all of a sudden, we come up with ideas, feelings, and actions that are exactly the opposite of wisdom or understanding. Discuss:

a. What are some of the ways in which your life reflects quick, often unexpected, shifts from understanding to lack of understanding?

b. What are some of the signs of the "side by side" appearance of wisdom and foolishness in your family and family lifestyle? your school and church? your community and society at large?

2. After his question of **3:13** James appeals to his readers to live fruitfully by faith in Christ. Just as you can identify a tree by the fruit it produces, so you identify a person of godly wisdom by the way he or she talks and acts. When James says that a wise and understanding person should show his good life by his works in the humility that comes from wisdom (**3:13**), how does that relate to what he wrote in **2:14–26?**

Other Examples (Besides You)

1. How does Abraham (2:21) serve as a good example? What seemed to be unwise about God's instruction to Abraham to sacrifice his son Isaac and Abraham's setting out to do that? What was the "wisdom of God" in this matter? What was the wisdom of Abraham (2:22–23)?

2. How did Abraham's action show a work of faith done in "the humility that comes from wisdom" (3:13)?

3. Can you explain to someone else how Rahab (2:25; Joshua 2:4, 15; 6:17) is also a good example of the type of person that James in 3:13 encourages his hearers to be? What in her actions might have appeared to be unwise or simply foolish? Using Rahab as an example, how would you explain 3:13 in relation to 2:22?

4. Can you give examples of the wisdom of Christian people with whom you are acquainted? Could someone else refer to you as such an example? Why or why not?

Wisdom from Below

1. Compare the characteristics of an unwise, envious person **(3:14–16)** with the "humility that comes from wisdom" **(3:13)**. Envy is always related to selfishness. What is the connection between feelings of envy and selfish ambition **(3:14)** and the temptation to become judgmental or partial in our dealings with others **(2:4)?**

2. James writes that a person who has bitter envy and selfish ambition in his heart should not boast **(3:14)**. Would such boasting be like the boasting of **1:9** or of **3:5?** Why do envy and selfish ambition always "deny the truth" **(3:14)?**

3. James says that this false wisdom that comes out of envy or ambition does not "come down from heaven" **(3:15).** What kind of wisdom is it then? See **1:16–17.** What does that judgment on self-made virtue say about all of the "goodness" we try to create ourselves?

4. Does your experience agree with James' statement in **3:16?** Can you give examples? How does this statement support what Jesus said in **Matthew 7:15–20?**

Wisdom from Above

1. By contrast with the negatives in **3:13–16** try to determine the meaning of the characteristics of "the wisdom that comes from heaven" in **verses 17–18.** First of all, it is pure. What is the meaning of "pure" **(3:17)?** Check the positive statements in **1:1, 18; 2:1, 23.** See also **Romans 14:20** and **Philippians 4:8.** How is our wisdom and our self made pure **(Romans 5:1)?**

2. Wisdom that comes from above is peace-loving **(3:17).** What do the following passages say about a peacemaker: **Matthew 5:9; Isaiah 32:17; Hebrews 12:11?**

3. Godly wisdom is considerate. Is a wise person "open-minded"? In what way? How is closed-mindedness and refusal to hear others **(1:19)** a sign of jealousy and selfishness **(3:16)?** How is being "open to reason" different from being "double-minded" **(1:8)?**

4. The wisdom that comes from heaven is considerate, submissive. What is the relationship between being considerate and submissive to acting out of godly wisdom **(3:13)?**

5. Godly wisdom is merciful. How do you relate "full of mercy" to James' statement in **2:13?**

6. Wisdom from heaven is impartial and sincere. In what way are the words "impartial" and "sincere" defined by what James says in **1:2–4,** but a contrast to his description of the person in **1:5–8?**

The Word for Us

1. **James 3:18** promises a "harvest of righteousness" to those who have the wisdom to "sow in peace." What are some practical things you can do to grow in godly wisdom?

2. Sadly, we are unable to measure up to James' standard of wisdom. What should be our response when confronted with words that not only condemn us but also hold up ideals we cannot attain?

3. Read **Romans 7:21–8:1.** How is Paul's struggle to attain perfection like ours? What is his solution when he cannot produce the goodness he seeks? Where will we, then, finally find wisdom?

Closing

Pray together the words of "I Pray You, Dear Lord Jesus."

I pray You, dear Lord Jesus,
My heart to keep and train
That I Your holy temple
From youth to age remain.
Oh, turn my thoughts forever
From worldly wisdom's lore;
If I but learn to know You,
I shall not want for more.

Lesson 9

Love of the World and Love of God (James 4:1–10)

Theme Verse

"Submit yourselves, then, to God. Resist the devil, and he will flee from you" **(James 4:7).**

Goal

That we might recognize that our conflicts and argumentative spirit stem from our sinful nature and turn in repentance to God, who will forgive us for Jesus' sake and renew us with His Spirit.

What's Going On Here?

"What causes fights and quarrels among you?" James asks. Apparently, the early Christian community struggled with the same problems that surface in the church today: quarreling, backbiting, feuding, judging. James puts his finger on the root of the problem by answering his own question. It is the sinful desires that battle within us that cause our troubles.

James' call to repentance is clear: turn from your sinful ways, from friendship with the world, which is hatred toward God, and resist the devil. Come back to God in penitence; He will welcome you with open arms.

James' words are meant for us too. Whenever we find ourselves caught up in arguments and backbiting in our personal or church relationships, we too need to examine our hearts, confess our sinfulness, and ask God for forgiveness and renewal.

Searching the Scriptures
Seen Any Good Wars Lately?

1. We are never free from the passions "that battle" within us **(4:1)**. What do James' words in **verses 1–2** have to say to our attempts to discount our conflicts with others as "little disagreements" or "minor conflicts"? Are conflicts ever minor?

2. In **verse 2** James talks about coveting or wanting something we can't get. What do the Ninth and Tenth Commandments have to say about this kind of desire? (See **Exodus 20:17.**) Is desiring always wrong? (See **1 Peter 2:2.**)

3. We expect to see a child becoming angry and striking back. We say he is being "childish." What words do you use, however, when you describe similar actions in another adult? (immature, impatient, quick temper?) What words do you use when you happen to observe such actions in yourself? (righteous anger, defending your rights, bold diplomacy?) Why the difference? What does the difference say about our own inability to face our sin?

4. "You want something but don't get it. You kill and covet" (4:2). Those are harsh, condemning words. Does evil desire lead to killing? How? Compare **Matthew 5:21–22.** How does James' condemnation of coveting and killing (4:2) also help to explain **1:22–23, 26; 2:4, 14–15?**

Mirror, Mirror on the Wall

1. How do **verses 2b** and **3** convict us of breaking God's law? To which commandments does James refer?

2. Asking comes up often in the New Testament. Read **Matthew 7:7; John 11:22; 16:22–23.** The implication of the passages is that God will give us what we ask for. Why don't the people to whom James writes get what they want? How do they "ask with wrong motives" **(James 4:3)?** What do **John 14:13** and **John 15:7** have to say about their problem?

3. The selfish life **(4:2–3)** is a total compromise of one's faith in God. It is a life of friendship to the world and hostility against God **(4:4).** Why cannot one be a friend of God and also a friend of the world? Look at Jesus' words **(Matthew 16:24)** for your answer.

God's Heartache

1. Who or what is the "spirit" of **4:5?**

2. Does **verse 6** mean that God is more generous with those who earn His favor by being humble? Read **Romans 5:20.** Does the passage indicate that God gives more grace because we need it or because we earn it?

3. From **4:1–6** can you characterize the proud and the humble? What has James written before about God's relationship with the humble (**1:9; 2:5**)?

Draw Near to God

1. **4:7** connects directly with **verse 4.** It is in separating from the world that we submit to God. Do we have the power to resist Satan on our own? According to **1 Peter 5:8–10** who is this devil? What are his weapons? How are we able to resist?

2. The Old Testament connections are strong in **4:7–10.** The phrase "come near to God" is from Old Testament worship. See **Exodus 19:10; Leviticus 11:44; Psalm 19:12;** and **51:10.** The exhortation to "grieve, mourn, and wail" in repentance also has Old Testament roots **(Psalm 38:6; Isaiah 38:14).** Since James is addressing Jewish Christians, what impact would his frequent appeal to the Old Testament have on them? How does it impact you?

3. What has God promised to the humble that is truly a reason for joy and laughter? See **Isaiah 55:7** and **Acts 2:38.** Finally all of the commands and promises again come together in the Gospel promise of salvation in Jesus Christ.

The Word for Us

1. Read **4:1–10** aloud again. How do the accusations of these verses and the rest of the epistle make you feel?

2. Is the purpose of James' words in this section to make us try harder to be good? Why is that not possible? How does James show that the Law accuses us and sends us to the cross of Christ for forgiveness?

3. Think of two or three people with whom you are having conflict at this time. List some concrete things you can do to restore these relationships in a God-pleasing manner.

Closing

Speak or sing stanzas 1 and 3 of "God of Grace and God of Glory."

God of grace and God of Glory,
On Your people pour Your pow'r;
Crown Your ancient church's story;
Bring its bud to glorious flow'r.
Grant us wisdom, grant us courage
For the facing of this hour,
For the facing of this hour.

Cure Your children's warring madness;
Bend our pride to Your control;
Shame our wanton, selfish gladness,
Rich in things and poor in soul.
Grant us wisdom, grant us courage
Lest we miss Your kingdom's goal,
Lest we miss Your kingdom's goal.

Lesson 10

What Is Your Life?
(James 4:11–17)

Theme Verse

"If it is the Lord's will, we will live and do this" **(James 4:15)**.

Goal

That we may forsake spiritual arrogance and remember to rely on God for all that we do and say.

What's Going On Here?

Too often today, just as in James' day, Christians live as though God is not in the picture. They fail to recognize God's providential care for them or appreciate His blessings in their lives. Instead, they act as if they are self-sufficient and in control of their future. They sit in judgment on their brother and take credit for all their successes **(4:11, 16)**.

James tells us that this is not only foolish but sinful. For after all, we do not even know what will happen tomorrow! He points us back to God, who has given us life and sustains it. James reminds us that it is the Lord who directs our lives for His good purpose. We are to remain faithful and trust in Him for all that we do and say.

Searching the Scriptures
Brother

1. In his epistle what is the bond to which James appeals whenever he uses the word "brother"? See **1:2.** Why would an appeal to their brother-

hood be particularly meaningful to those who were dispersed?

2. What does a change from a brotherly to an unbrotherly attitude say? Do we ever have the privilege of being unbrotherly? What does Jesus say in **Matthew 5:43–47?**

A Judge! Who, Me?

1. Reread **James 4:11.** When one person speaks evil against and judges another, the law does not permit him to escape condemnation. What is James' line of reasoning in this verse?

2. **Verse 12** suggests that we actually are putting ourself in the place of God when we judge and condemn. What is the correct way to handle the faults of others **(Luke 17:4; Ephesians 4:32; Colossians 3:13.** Compare **Matthew 18:15–17.)?**

3. What is the connection between **4:12** and **2:12–13?**

Let's Make Some Money!

1. James continues his criticism of spiritual arrogance and evil-mindedness in verses **13–17.** He also continues his encouragement to be faithful and to trust in the Lord for all that we do and say. Does James condemn making money? Does he criticize a person's making a profit in his business? What fault is he focusing on in **4:13–17?**

2. How does James' criticism apply to us today? Give an example. Can you give an example from your own life of your making plans without any thought to God?

3. Compare the accusing question in **4:12** (Who are you ?) with that of **4:14** (What is your life ... ?). Are the questions similar? What kind of answer do they seek? What does the answer say about us?

4. Here James compares life to a "mist" or vapor. The statement would have had immediate relationship for the Hebrew reader with **Ecclesiastes**. In that Old Testament wisdom book, with many similarities to **James,** the word translated "vanity" is used often. The Hebrew idea in the word was "vapor" or "breath." What do the first few verses of **Ecclesiastes** say to enhance James' argument here? Compare **Luke 12:16–21.**

If It Is the Lord's Will

1. Instead of arrogantly bragging and playing God in our lives **(4:16)**, how ought Christians to plan and live **(4:15)**?

2. What does James mean by the statement "if it is the Lord's will, we will live"? What is the Lord's will for us? How do the following passages help you to answer that question: **2 Peter 3:9; Luke 21:18?** See also **James 1:18** and **3:17–18.**

The Word for Us

1. Discuss ways to improve our ability to include God in our planning. Is just saying "if it is the Lord's will" **(4:15)** enough? In what other ways should God be involved as we think about tomorrow, or next week, or next year? See **Matthew 24:45–46** and **25:14–30.**

2. What part does prayer play in our planning? How about worship? Forgiveness? Can you come up with specific suggestions for Christian planning?

3. In **verse 17** James says that anyone who knows what he ought to do but doesn't do it, sins. Where in your life are you failing to do what you should? Where does forgiveness come in? List several things you can do with the Spirit's help to improve.

Closing

Heavenly Father, You have created us and redeemed us as Your own through Jesus. Because of You alone we live and move and have our being. Keep us mindful of You and Your blessings so that we do not forget about You or think we are in charge of our own destiny. Guide and govern us by Your Word and Spirit so that we may know and do Your will as we go about our daily life. In Jesus' name, we ask this. Amen.

Lesson 11

The Love of Money
(James 5:1–6)

Theme Verse

"Listen, you rich people, weep … because of the misery that is coming upon you" **(James 5:1)**.

Goal

That we might learn to recognize the pitfalls of riches and appreciate that our true wealth and blessing lie in being right with God through faith in Christ Jesus.

What's Going On Here?

In this section of his epistle, James like the prophets of the Old Testament pronounces woe on those who find ultimate worth in wealth and the power it brings. In pursuit of their own selfish lifestyles they manipulate, cheat—even murder—others. James says their money will be worthless at Christ's return and announces the coming misery and judgment of God on their sinfulness. These verses are also a reminder to us to measure our wealth by God's standards and to spend time accumulating the treasures that are worthwhile in God's Kingdom.

Searching the Scriptures
How Now

1. The rich whom James addresses in the first **six verses** of **chapter 5** are probably either (1) nonbelievers altogether, or (2) people formerly Christians who have fallen from faith in Christ because of their love of

wealth. The second group is more likely since nonbelievers would have little interest in James' words. In either case, how does **5:1–6** serve as a warning for all?

2. Which expressions of judgment suggest the last judgment at the time of Christ's final coming?

3. In what way do these statements of judgment suggest that the rich are deceived in their security in riches **(vv. 1–3)?**

How Are You Doing?

1. In what way do possessions tend to be a false security for you? What things in particular tempt you to put confidence in them? What false securities characterize our society in general? Do you think that riches, or the love of money, characterize us as a people and nation? Are we a godly people? Are there any such false securities that may be operating in your congregation, school, or national church body?

2. Does the contrast between the rich and the poor as given in **5:1–6** apply today? Give an example. Do the rich still rob the poor? How about the poor who steal from the rich because the rich can afford it? Is the love of money confined to any one economic class? Explain.

Self-Deception and Judgment

1. Although not always apparent at first glance, the expectation of the end time or final judgment (the "eschatological") is an underlying dimension of James' epistle. In what way do the words "rotted" and "eaten" **(5:2)** refer to the end time? See **Job 13:28.**

2. James writes that the corrosion of silver and gold will be evidence against the rich **(5:3).** What do you suppose James means by silver and gold corroding?

3. What is the only wealth or treasure that will be of value on the last day? See **Matthew 6:19–21.** How do we lay up treasure in heaven?

Champion of the Oppressed

1. Have you ever had to wait unduly long to be paid for your work or been cheated out of your pay? How does that feel? James is certain that God hears the cries of the harvesters who have been defrauded **(5:4)**. The theme of God's protection for the oppressed is familiar in Scripture. See **Deuteronomy 24:14–15; Genesis 21:15–21; Luke 16:19–26.** What does that say about the love of God?

2. James' words in **5:5**, "you have fattened yourselves in the day of slaughter," might also have brought words of Old Testament Scripture to mind. How does Jeremiah's use of the word "slaughter" **(Jeremiah 25:34)** help to explain the words of judgment in **James 5:5–6?**

3. What contrast do you find in the example of the Suffering Servant of **Isaiah 53?**

The Lord Hears

1. The "resource" for the righteous and the poor person is the Lord Himself. The cries of the victims of unrighteousness, of injustice, reach the ears of the Lord **(5:4)**. In what way does **Galatians 6:7** apply both to the rich and also to the poor?

2. There are a number of statements in Scripture, in the prophecies of the new Kingdom of God to come, about the Lord's care for the poor and all those treated unjustly. One of the better known is Isaiah **11:1–5.** You might also look up **Isaiah 5:16–17; 9:7; 25:4; and 35** as a start to see how many others you can find.

3. Compare the characteristics of the sinfully rich in **James 5:1–6** with the characteristics of the Kingdom of God, the ministry of Jesus, and of the people in the Kingdom of God. Are they the same or opposite?

The Word for Us

1. In the light of these words and of Jesus' comment in **Matthew 19:24,** is it possible for rich people to be saved? Why is it difficult?

2. Are we rich? How can we be on guard against becoming trapped by our possessions?

3. Can you think of specific ways possessions can be made to serve us and Christ's Kingdom and not vice versa?

4. What does it mean to hold all our blessings from God—family, home, job, possessions, wealth—with open hands (instead of a tight grip)? Why is this important?

Closing

Ask a participant to close the session in prayer or sing together stanza 3 of "What Is the World to Me."

The world seeks after wealth
And all that mammon offers
Yet never is content
Though gold should fill its coffers.
I have a higher good,
Content with it I'll be:
My Jesus is my wealth.
What is the world to me!

Lesson 12

Living Expectantly
(James 5:7–12)

Theme Verse

"Be patient, then, brothers, until the Lord's coming" **(James 5:7).**

Goal

That we may by the Spirit's power develop patience and perseverance amid our struggles and remain firm in our faith in Jesus.

What's Going On Here?

In these verses James reminds us of a number of truths he has previously treated: (1) We are to be patient and view our struggles here in light of our eternal destination; (2) We can trust God to give us good gifts; and (3) We are to view our trials as opportunities through which God draws us closer to Him rather than turning against Him and our fellow believer in grumbling and strife.

Searching the Scriptures
What Is Your Hope?

1. What does the word "patient" mean in **5:7?** Why does James consider "the Lord's coming" a reason for patient living now?

2. At Christ's final coming, a believer in Jesus Christ shall experience more fully what he or she now possesses. Read **James 5** and list all the words and phrases that either directly or indirectly refer to the final coming of the Lord.

3. Which ones suggest judgment and punishment? Which ones suggest promise and the fulfillment of life?

4. Relate the words and phrases you have found to the Law, which accuses and threatens, and to the Gospel, which frees us.

5. Pressured by whatever difficulties they may have, such as being oppressed and exploited by the rich **(5:1–6),** believers might be tempted to forget about God and think that there is no future. How does James' encouragement in **5:7** apply in such an instance?

A Future with Meaning

1. James' tells his readers to be patient—to trust patiently in God. James' example of the farmer (5:7) illustrates a present, expectant hope. What is the farmer's expectation when he sows the seed? Is that expectation a hopeless hope or a meaningful hope? Why? Explain how the farmer's present activity and his hope for the future are interrelated.

2. To stand firm (5:8) is the same as to be steadfast in one's faith in Christ (1:3–4). A contrast is to waver (1:6) and to be double-minded (1:7–8). Can a person stand firm by himself?

3. How does James' statement "the Lord's coming is near" (5:8) explain the meaning of his encouragement to "stand firm"? Compare 1:12.

The Yes of Faith

1. James says "the Lord's coming is near" (5:8) and "the Judge is standing at the door" (5:9). Since Christ has not yet come, was James mistaken in his statements? Explain.

2. "Don't grumble against each other" **(5:9).** Are you a "grumbler" or a patient person? What kinds of situations tax your patience most? Are your times of impatience most related to personal troubles or to your relationship with others?

3. Describe Job's experience of suffering. How did he persevere? What did the Lord finally bring about for Job? How was the Lord "full of compassion and mercy" to him?

4. Read **Hebrews 11.** How do these heroes of faith (with Job) illustrate what James writes in **5:7–11?** How was each of them also a witness that "the Lord was full of compassion and mercy"?

5. Since you live expectantly by faith and hope in God, why is there no need to swear **(v. 12)?** Compare **verse 12** with **Matthew 5:34–37.**

The Word for Us

1. What difference does your expectation of the coming of the Lord make in your life day by day?

2. Think of people who are examples to you of patience and steadfastness, like the prophets of old? Can you pinpoint how they became patient and steadfast? If you are able, you may want to ask them.

3. Do other people see you as an example to them of a patient person rather than a grumbler? Why is it important for us to come often to the cross for forgiveness in order to be able to face our daily tasks with a positive confidence?

4. How would you encourage a person who was constantly complaining?

Closing

Sing or speak together stanzas 1 and 3 of "Jesus, Still Lead On."

Jesus, still lead on
Till our rest be won;
And although the way be cheerless,
We will follow calm and fearless;
Guide us by Your hand
To our fatherland.

When we seek relief
From a longfelt grief,
When temptations come alluring,
Make us patient and enduring;
Show us that bright shore
Where we weep no more.

Lesson 13

Personal Care—God's Care (James 5:13–20)

Theme Verse

"The prayer of a righteous man is powerful and effective" (**James 5:16**).

Goal

That we may truly value the gift of prayer and allow every aspect of our life—both suffering and joy—to be governed by God's Word and prayer.

What's Going On Here?

James concludes his epistle with a call to prayer along with caring concern for and loving actions towards the community of believers. He tells his fellow believers to pray during both troubled times and times of joy, for those who are sick, and for those who have fallen from the faith. Why? Because the prayers of those who believe in Jesus are powerful and effective. God, of course, does not promise to answer yes to all of our prayers. But He does delight in responding to them in love according to His will and to use them to accomplish His good purposes.

Searching the Scriptures

Me, a "Minister"?

1. Compare **5:13–20** and **2:14–18.** In what way is our personal "min-

istry" a Christian witness to our faith?

2. Why is it important to cultivate a caring ministry for each other?

Up and At It!

1. How does your faith-life show in your ministry to others especially to those who are troubled **(5:13)**, the sick **(5:14)**, the erring **(5:20)?**

2. We know that both bad times and good times can be occasions to fall into sin. When we suffer, we may become angry with God or feel far from Him. When things are good, we might think we don't need Him. How does **James 5:13–17** speak to this situation?

3. What is our real solution for doubt or weak faith? How does prayer enter in?

For the Sick in Body or Spirit

1. The "elders" **(v. 14)** to whom James refers were overseers of the "pastoral ministry" in a community of believers. Is such calling on the sick limited only to the elders, or are all Christians involved to one extent or another?

2. If a sick person should pray to the Lord, why should he also call on the "elders of the church" to pray for him **(5:14)**?

3. What is meant by the phrase "anoint him with oil" **(5:14)**? Do you think that the anointing with oil is devotional, medicinal, or both? See **Leviticus 8:12; 1 Samuel 16:13; Isaiah 1:6; Mark 6:13; Luke 10:34.**

4. What is the "prayer offered in faith" **(5:15)** that will save the sick man? James says (1) "the prayer offered in faith will make the sick person well" and (2) "the Lord will raise him up." What is the cause of the healing—prayer, faith, or the Lord? How are the three related? See **1:17–18.**

Prayer

1. "Healing" and "forgiveness" often go together in Scripture. See **Matthew 9:1–12.** In **5:16,** is the healing physical or spiritual, or both? How does James' statement in **5:16** bring both together?

2. In what way is Elijah a good model of confident prayer and God's answer (**1 Kings 17:1; 18:1, 41**)?

3. Look up the following passages, which contain the Lord's invitation to us to pray and His promise to hear us: **Luke 11:1–13; Matthew 6:5–15; John 16:23–24.** If our prayers seem to go unanswered, does that mean there is something wrong with the prayer? our faith? What might God be telling us?

4. To bring someone back to faith in Christ, after he has wandered away from the truth (**5:19–20**), is literally to save a person from death. How is our ministry to our straying brothers and sisters best accomplished? What is needed—Law or Gospel? How?

The Word for Us

1. Read through your church bulletin or worship folder for any Sunday. How do they compare? Do people who come into contact with your congregation encounter a group of caring, concerned people like those described in James? Why or why not? What resources do you have to help your congregation become more like James' ideal?

2. When God chooses not to answer prayer the way we want or as soon as we want, what could be the reason?

3. How can your church better encourage and support the prayer life of its members?

4. What have been the main benefits for you in this book? List ways to implement with the Spirit's help two or three things you have learned.

5. Can you work out a strategy for spiritual growth in your life and congregation that would allow the kind of spiritual growth James encourages? What element is most important in that strategy?

Closing

Sing or speak together stanzas 1–2, and 6 of "Come, My Soul, with Every Care."

Come, my soul, with ev'ry care,
Jesus loves to answer prayer;
He Himself bids you to pray,
Therefore will not turn away.

You are coming to your King,
Large petitions with you bring;
For His grace and pow'r are such
None can ever ask too much.

Show me what I am to do;
Ev'ry hour my strength renew.
Let me live a life of faith;
Let me die Your people's death.

JAMES
How Faith Works

Leaders Notes

Preparing to Teach James

In preparation to teach, consult the introduction to the book of James in the *Concordia Self-Study Bible,* and if possible, read the *Concordia Self-Study Commentary* (CPH, 1979).

Also read the text in a modern translation. The NIV is generally referred to in the lesson comments.

In the section "Searching the Scriptures" the leader guides discussion, using the questions given (or others) to help the class discover what the text actually says. This is a major part of teaching, namely, directing the learners to discover for themselves.

Another major portion of each lesson is "The Word for Us." This section helps participants, through discussion, to see the meaning of the text for our times, for the church and world today, and especially for our own lives.

Group Bible Study

Group Bible study means mutual learning from one another under the guidance of a leader or facilitator. The Bible is an inexhaustible resource. No one person can discover all it has to offer. In a class many eyes see many things and can apply them to many life situations. The leader should resist the temptation to "give the answers" and so act as an "authority." This teaching approach stifles participation by individual members and can actually hamper learning. As a general rule the teacher is not to "give interpretation" but to "develop interpreters." Of course, there are times when the leader should and must share insights and information gained by his or her own deeper research. The ideal class is one in which the leader guides class members through the lesson and engages them in meaningful sharing and discussion at all points, leading them to a summary of the lesson at the close. As a general rule, don't explain what the learners can discover by themselves.

Have a chalkboard and chalk or newsprint and marking pens available to emphasize significant points of the lesson. Put your inquiries or the inquiries of participants into questions, problems, or issues. This provokes thought. Keep discussion to the point. List on the chalkboard or newsprint the answers given. Then determine the most vital points made in the discussion. Ask additional questions to fill apparent gaps.

The aim of every Bible study is to help people grow spiritually, not merely in biblical and theological knowledge, but in Christian thinking and living. This means growth in Christian attitudes, insights, and skills for Christian living. The focus of this course must be the church and the world of our day. The guiding question will be, "What does the Lord teach us for life today through the book of James?"

Pace Your Teaching

Do not try to cover every question in each lesson. This will lead to undue haste and frustration. Be selective. Pace your teaching. Spend no more than five to 10 minutes with the "Theme Verse," "Goal," and "What's Going On Here?". Take time to go into the text by topic, but not word by word. Get the sweep of meaning. Occasionally stop to help the class gain understanding of a word or concept. Allow approximately 10 to 15 minutes for "The Word for Us." Spending approximately five minutes for "Closing" and announcements, you will notice, allows you only approximately 30 minutes for "Searching the Scriptures."

Should your group have more than a one-hour class period, you can take it more leisurely. But do not allow any lesson to "drag" and become tiresome. Keep it moving. Keep it alive. Keep it meaningful. Eliminate some questions and restrict yourself to those questions most meaningful to the members of the class. If most members study the text at home, they can report their findings, and the time gained can be applied to relating the lesson to life.

Good Preparation

Good preparation by the leader usually affects the pleasure and satisfaction the class will experience.

Suggestions to the Leader for Using the Study Guide
The Lesson Pattern

This set of 13 lessons is based on a significant and timely New Testament book—James. The material is designed to aid Bible study, that is, to aid a consideration of the written Word of God, with discussion and personal application growing out of the text at hand.

The typical lesson is divided into six sections:
1. Theme Verse
2. Goal
3. What's Going On Here?
4. Searching the Scriptures
5. The Word for Us
6. Closing

"Theme Verse," "Goal," and "What's Going On Here?" give the leader assistance in arousing the interest of the group in the concepts taught in the session. Do not linger too long over the introductory remarks. Show that the verses to be studied are meaningful to Christian faith and life today.

"Searching the Scriptures" provides the real "spade work" necessary for Bible study. Here the class digs, uncovers, and discovers; it gets the facts and observes them. Comment from the leader is needed only to the extent that it helps the group understand the text. The same is true of looking up the indicated parallel passages. The questions in the study guide, arranged under subheadings and corresponding to sections within the text, are intended to help the participants discover the meaning of the text.

Having determined what the text says, the class is ready to apply the message. Having heard, read, marked, and learned the Word of God, proceed to digest it inwardly through discussion, evaluation, and application. This is done, as the study guide suggests, by taking the truths found in James and applying them to the world and Christianity, in general, and then to personal Christian life. Class time may not permit discussion of all questions and topics. In preparation the leader may need to select two or three and focus on them. These questions bring God's message to the individual Christian. Close the session by reviewing one important truth from the lesson.

Remember, the Word of God is sacred, but the study guide is not. The guide offers only suggestions. The leader should not hesitate to alter the guidelines or substitute others to meet his or her needs and the needs of the participants. Adapt your teaching plan to your class and your class period. Good teaching directs the learner to discover for himself or herself. For the teacher this means directing the learner, not giving the learner answers. As you prepare, mark those sections that suggest a class activity. Choose the verses that should be looked up in Scripture. What discussion questions will you ask? at what points? Write them in the margin of your study guide. Involve class members, but give them clear directions. What practical actions will you propose for the week following the lesson? Having class members hold each other accountable for using their tongues to build up others? Making a plan to resolve a conflict with another church member? Talking about injustice to a county or city administrator? Which of the items do you consider most important for your class?

How will you best use your teaching period? Do you have 45 minutes? an hour? or 1½ hours? If time is short, what should you cut? Learn to become a wise steward of class time.

Be sure to take time to summarize the lesson, or have a class member do it. Plan brief opening and closing devotions using members of the class. Suggestions are provided in this Leaders Notes.

Lesson 1
A Greeting to Some Special Slaves (James 1:1)

Before the Session

Ask the Lord to bless your preparation as you begin to study His Word through James. Take time to read through the entire book. Consult several good commentaries as well. You do not need to "know all the answers," but the class will look to you as a resource person for the discussion.

The Class Session

Open the class with prayer. Allow some time at the beginning of this first session for the participants to become acquainted with each other. Allow each person a little time to tell something about himself/herself. Keep the atmosphere informal. Set the tone of acceptance so that people will be encouraged to participate in the class discussions.

Then check to see that everyone has a Bible and ask a member of the class to read aloud the "Theme Verse," "Goal," and "What's Going On Here?" in the study guide. Ask for questions or comments. You might want to supplement the information in the study guide with some of the following information:

The book of James was likely one of the earliest of all the New Testament writings, probably written before A.D. 50. After Stephen's martyrdom **(Acts 7:55–8:3),** Christian believers from the early Jerusalem church were scattered throughout the Roman world due to increased persecution. As leader of the Jerusalem church, James wrote to instruct and encourage his dispersed people who had been cut off from the support of Christian churches and were facing various trials.

The distinctive characteristics of this letter include (1) its Jewish nature, (2) its emphasis on a living faith characterized by good deeds that reflect lifestyles consistent with God's Word, (3) its simple organization, (4) its familiarity with Jesus' teachings in the Sermon on the Mount, (5) its similarities with Old Testament wisdom literature such as Proverbs, and (6) its excellent Greek (*Concordia Self-Study Bible*, p. 1897).

Searching the Scriptures

Read aloud or have volunteers read aloud the suggested portions of Scripture before discussing the questions. You may wish to have participants discuss the questions in small groups, if your class is large. Or if time is limited, consider dividing the class into two groups and assigning each group alternating sections. If you divide your class into small groups, allow time for groups to share the answers to the questions with the entire class.

About the Greeting

1–3. **Verse 1** contains all the direct information we have about the author of the epistle, i.e., a servant of Jesus Christ. The same statement of identity can also be made about us, because the Holy Spirit has brought us to faith in Jesus Christ as Savior.

The words "servant" and "slave" have a different meaning, each depending on our relationship to God and our fellow human being. In popular love songs, a person may refer to himself as a slave to the one he loves. A slave can serve in joyful love and devotion, but slavery can also be miserable. With respect to the Law, which convicts us of our sinfulness, the words "servant" and "slave" are negative. We are slaves to sin, angry because in our sinfulness we are reluctant "slaves" and enemies of God. But under the Gospel of forgiveness we are the redeemed and reconciled people of God. He is our Father, Brother, Helper, to whom in love and devotion we offer ourselves as His servants. It is to the childlike servants of a loving Father that James addresses this epistle.

4. In **Matt. 16:16; John 6:68–69;** and **1 Cor. 12:3,** we focus on the name "Christ," "Lord," and "Jesus." Notice that the person Jesus is called "Christ." The Greek word *Christos* means "Anointed," the same as the Hebrew word *Messiah*. The disciples confessed that the man Jesus was also the Christ, the Son of God, who had come to be the Savior **(Matt. 1:21–23)** and Lord. Look at the Second Article of the Apostles' Creed (and the Nicene Creed) as a summary of Christian teaching about Jesus as Savior.

To Whom Was James Written?

1–2. For background on "dispersed," see **Esther 3:8; Is. 11:12; Ezek. 12:15; John 7:35; 1 Peter 1:1, 17; 2:11; Heb. 11:13–16.** Note that "dispersion" (and also "twelve tribes") can have a literal meaning: Israel and Judah being sent into captivity for their unfaithfulness to God. It also can have figurative meanings: (1) Believers in every place (the universal church) under persecution or otherwise. (2) Believers who see themselves as wayfarers on earth until Christ takes them to their real home at His final coming. It is to the persecuted wayfarers and to the scattered Jews that the epistle was written.

Is It Really a Letter?

1. Because of the word "greeting" in **verse 1,** the epistle of James is accepted as a letter. The word "greeting" was a common form of salutation

in the first centuries of the church and still is among some people. The basic meaning of the word is to "be glad," "to rejoice."

2. Most scholars agree that the body of the material is not a letter. By contrast **3 John** is much more letterlike: It is directly personal, includes references to contemporary people, events, and plans, and at the conclusion, it includes personal greetings from the writer and others.

3. The style of **James** indicates that it is more a series of sermonettes on various themes written from a pastoral heart. James' purpose is to teach and encourage his dispersed people who are undergoing various trials to live their faith in word and deeds.

Who Really Wrote James?

1–4. Read the study guide material and research the passages. The author identifies himself as James **(1:1)**. There are four men in the New Testament named James but most likely the writer of this epistle was James, the brother of Jesus. The writer could not have been the apostle James since he died in A.D. 44, a date much too early for him to have written this letter. The other two men named James were not well known or influential enough to have written this epistle.

At first, James did not believe in Jesus **(John 7:5)**. Later, he became prominent in the church at Jerusalem. Christ appeared to him after His resurrection **(Acts 1:14; 1 Cor. 15:7)**. James was a leader in the Jerusalem council **(Acts 15:4, 13–19)**. Paul met to confer with James on visits to Jerusalem **(Acts 21:17–18; Gal. 1:18–19)**. In **Gal. 2:9** Paul calls James a "pillar" of the church.

The Word for Us

1–5. Help the class personalize the meaning of the concept of "slavery to God." Use the passages and input from the class to summarize the meaning of "slavery" and to show how our slavery to God is freedom in that it frees us from slavery to ourselves. Help participants think of practical, concrete ways to serve God and others. Remind participants that God purchased us back from our slavery to sin through the blood of His only Son shed on the cross. God's great love for us in Christ Jesus motivates us to serve others. Christ became enslaved by our sin so that we might be freed from sin to serve Him.

Closing

Ask participants for prayer concerns or requests. Include these requests as you pray the closing prayer in the study guide.

Lesson 2

Joy in the Midst of Joylessness (James 1:2–8)

Before the Session

Read **James 1:2–8.** Read through the study guide material and check out some good Bible commentaries on these verses.

The Class Session

Ask for a volunteer to begin today's class with prayer. Have someone read the "Theme Verse," "Goal," and "What's Going On Here?" in the study guide.

Before beginning your Scripture study, draw two columns on a chalkboard. Label one "Joy" and the other one "Trials." Ask participants to list moments of joy under the one column and examples of trials under the other. Use class input and come to an agreement, based on the examples shared, of definitions for each word. Can any of the trials listed be an occasion for joy? Why is it usually difficult to respond to trials with joy? Use this discussion to lead into your study of the text.

Searching the Scriptures

Why Joy Is Real

1. The meaning of the selected words and phrases of **verses 1–6** is clear from James' text. They draw attention to the underlying unity of Christian thought in James' epistle. James' epistle has been dismissed as being too much Law (Luther) and as a collection of moral encouragements and wisdom sayings, containing very little "theology." The theology is there but much of it is indirectly expressed—some is assumed. The reference to God and Jesus Christ **(v. 1)**, for instance, points to the Trinity. God's mercy and grace are suggested in the statement about God's generous giving **(v. 5)**. The words "servant" **(v. 1)** and "my brothers" **(v. 2)** bring to mind the fellowship of saints, or the church. The relationship of a believer to God and the invitation to pray, believing God's promises to hear **(v. 6)** are further examples of the distinct Christian thought underlying and unifying the entire epistle.

2. Christians can continue to experience joy in trial as they find assurance in the promise that nothing "will be able to separate us from the love of God that is in Christ Jesus our Lord" **(Romans 8:39).**

Are You As Lonely As You Feel?

1–2. A person does not have to live long to realize that trials do not have to be sought, and that loneliness is a part of the experience. Trials inevitably come as a result of the evil in the world and our sinfulness. In addition to the external trials that come and the temptations of our own sinfulness, there are the "trials" that come from our serving the Lord and following Him **(Mark 8:34–38).** For instance, the opposition we experience for the stance we take and choices we make by faith in Jesus Christ can cause us to experience trials.

3. When James says to consider it "pure joy" when we face trials, he does not mean that because we are Christians we only find joy in troubles or that we are euphorically happy all the time. Rather, the Christian's joy is not dependent on circumstances. It denotes an attitude of trust founded on what Christ has done for us at the cross. It allows us to "rejoice" in our suffering because through it we know that God, who loves us, will work good.

Why Tests?

1–3. Focus on the patience we learn through trials, the victory we are promised and the confidence we can show in the face of trials by the grace of God in Jesus Christ. The parallel passages of **Rom. 5:1–6; 1 Peter 1:3–7; Heb. 12:7–11** do not necessarily suggest that writers borrowed from each other (a matter of dating the epistle). All the writers may have used material that was available to them in common from the sayings of Jesus, instructional material for Baptism, and the like.

Faith in Christ, Not Moralism

1–2. In teaching Christian faith and life, and the epistle of James, it is important that we do not teach God's Word and Christianity as another system of moral principles. James' epistle is not simply a moral treatise. Just to teach "a way of life" without reference to the Gospel of Jesus Christ is "moralizing." A Christian teacher can moralize without realizing it when he urges people to do or be good and fails to base it on God's Word of Law and Gospel. Moralizing is works righteousness. The perspective and focus for biblical teaching is to see how all Christian living springs from the Gospel as a fruit of faith in Christ—as opposed to the sinful "works" condemned by the Law.

Pray for Wisdom

1. Wise can mean intelligent, smart, capable, worldly, experienced, and the like. Here wisdom of Christian faith means not to waver as if one didn't know whom to trust, but to have the "faith-sense" to trust in God Himself. At times, not to waver may not be easy. It is comforting to know, though,

that the Holy Spirit Himself prays for us and that Jesus Christ, our Mediator and High Priest, hears those prayers of the Spirit on our behalf **(Rom. 8:26–27)**.

2. Although Luther could sharply criticize the epistle of James, he could also speak well of it. In his Large Catechism, on the last petition of the Lord's Prayer, Luther refers to these verses in James as an encouragement not to doubt, but to trust when we pray to God.

3. A double-minded person may also be one who feels that he is lost before he starts. In his double-mindedness he may be undecided as to whether he should ask God for help, or just give up to his loneliness and despair.

4–5. In **verses 2–8** James is being very realistic, even though it may sound idealistic. He has both feet on the ground. That is why James' encouragement to "consider it pure joy" **(1:2)** when a person meets trials is genuine.

Christianity is realistic. By God's grace through faith in Christ Jesus, the Christian knows the reality of Christ's death and resurrection for the forgiveness of sins and the victory of life. That is the practical realism of James' writing. Thus, James can write about the temptations to doubt, waver, and be double-minded. In the face of all trials, however, he encourages and strengthens his readers and hearers with the assurance of God's grace and the promise of God's leading them/us through temptations to the fullness of life in Him. There is indeed future in that!

The Word for Us

Discuss the questions in this section. Keep in mind the concluding thoughts for numbers 4–5 under "Pray for Wisdom" (above).

Closing

Pray together the prayer found in the study guide. Incorporate any prayer requests.

Lesson 3
Don't Blame God (James 1:9–15)

Before the Session

Read **James 1:9–15** and ask God to help you understand James' teaching here. Take time to read through the study guide material and leaders notes and meditate on God's Word.

The Class Session

Begin your class with prayer and take the opportunity to share some of the meaningful insights from last week's lesson. Ask someone to read the "Theme Verse," "Goal," and "What's Going On Here?" from the study guide. Read aloud **James 1:9–15.**

Searching the Scriptures

Just Who Are the Humble and the Rich?

1–5. John the Baptist serves as a good example of a humble person. Yet of him the Lord Jesus said that none was greater than he **(Luke 7:24–28).**

The humble or penitent person is lifted up, exalted, given a high position by God's grace and forgiveness. To be forgiven and to receive the benefits of Christ's death and victorious resurrection is to be given a high position or as some Bible translations have it: exalted. Our boasting is not the boasting of self-pride. It is the deep thankfulness, relief, and exaltation—regardless of what we may have economically and socially—of having the peace and the glory of being in the kingdom of God by faith in Jesus Christ.

The imagery of dying foliage to depict the life of man is ancient and traditional in both Biblical and non-Biblical literature. Additional passages in Scripture are **Job 14:2; Ps. 90:5; 102:4; Is. 40:6–8; 1 Peter 1:24.**

Interesting parallel passages about a humble-exalted person's "boast" in the Lord are Paul's statements about boasting in **2 Cor. 11:16–12:11** and **Phil. 3:3–7.**

Does It Make a Difference?

1–4. Use this section to talk about the meaning of "poverty" and "riches" in people's lives. Seek class participation and see if you can come to some kind of agreement as to what "humble circumstances" and "richness" mean today. Try to work with real feelings—platitudes in this area are easy (e.g., poverty is really a state of mind).

Do some Scriptural research on the terms.

A. A Christian's understanding of "humiliation" and "exaltation" is rooted in the scriptural framework of Law and Gospel, sin and grace, repentance and forgiveness.

B. Non-Christians usually define "humiliation" and "exaltation" in various moralistic ways. "Humble" might mean "debased," "modest," "keeping one's place," etc. "Exaltation" might mean "recognition … status," "popularity," etc. Each term fits into an individual's philosophy of life.

C. The humiliation of Jesus Christ refers to the fact that during the time between His conception and death Jesus did not always use His divine power or majesty. "And being found in appearance as a man, He humbled Himself and became obedient to death—even death on a cross" **(Phil. 2:8)**. Jesus' exaltation is the full use of His majesty beginning with His triumphal descent into hell and His continued full and constant use of that majesty now and in eternity. See **John 2:1–11, Luke 2:41–52, John 18:6,** and **Philippians 2:9–11**.

D. As the Holy Spirit convicts a person of his sinfulness through the Law **(John 16:8)**, and through the Gospel leads him to confess Christ as his Savior **(John 16:13–15; Rom. 1:16; 1 Cor. 12:3)**, the believer, by faith, affirms Scripture as the Word of God **(2 Tim. 3:14–17, 2 Peter 1:16–21)**. The proper distinction between Law and Gospel is the key that unlocks and makes the Holy Scriptures clear.

Getting Crowned

1. In **verse 12** the point of James' statement about enduring is not that a person earns a reward by enduring trials. That would be salvation by works. The point is that God Himself through Christ's death and resurrection offers us the gift of life and its fruitfulness. The "trial" is sin and Satan's attempt to snatch our faith and life in God away from us.

2. The end-time language of **chapter 1:7–8, 10–12, 15** should be emphasized and not overlooked. By faith in Jesus Christ a Christian possesses now as a gift of grace that which he shall experience in its revealed fullness at the final coming. The doctrine of the end time will be developed more fully in connection with **5:7–12** in lesson 12.

Does God Tempt Us

1–2. Lead the class in a discussion of temptation. Try to get an understanding of the difference between "trials" and "testing," which is God's work, and "tempting," in which Satan is at work.

3. In reference to temptation the Greek words for "dragged away" (ensnare) and "enticed" **(v. 14)** come from the world of hunting and fishing. The imagery suggests the bait that hunters use to lure an animal to a trap, and the bait that fishers use to entice a fish to grab the hook.

Use the remainder of the section to talk about individual temptations, as the participants are willing to share them. Try to make it more than a sharing of fears and failures but let those who are willing tell about the way in which their faith and faith life helps them to overcome temptation. Also, allow participants to share how God has used trials to strengthen their faith.

Give "Birth" to Death?

1. The irony is impressive. "Irony" refers to a surprising insight that comes in turn from an unexpected contrast with a biting (often satiric) twist. James returns to this imagery later in the epistle in the negative sense of useless **(2:20).** But in **chapter 1** he also develops its positive meaning when he writes about God's bringing believers forth as "a kind of firstfruits of all He created" **(v. 18).**

2–3. The first verse of this paragraph **(v. 12)** and the last verse **(v. 15)** make an effective contrast. Together they speak both sin and grace, Law and Gospel. Point out that death=Law and the crown of life offered to us by God's grace through faith in Christ Jesus=Gospel.

The Word for Us

Share responses to the discussion starters listed. Follow up on helpful suggestions regarding what the church can do to help members support each other in trials. Report to the group any significant actions that may be implemented due to their input. End by reminding members that it is not what we do but whose we are that is of eternal significance. Remind participants that by the power of the Holy Spirit working through God's Word, God does protect and defend us against all temptations. Faith strengthened by the Holy Spirit working through God's Word empowers and enables us to withstand temptations.

Closing

Ask participants for prayer concerns and requests. Close by speaking or singing together stanza 5 of " 'Come, Follow Me,' Said Christ, the Lord."

Lesson 4
True Religion (James 1:16–27)

Before the Session

Read **James 1:16–27,** the study materials, and leaders notes. Pray for God's blessing on your class and preparation.

The Class Session

Begin your class with prayer. Ask someone to read the "Theme Verse," "Goal," and "What's Going On Here?" from the study guide.

Engage class members in a brief discussion of the meaning of the word *true*. Ask them, "Do you trust the word *true*? If after you enter a place of business, someone would come up to you and say that he could show you the "true" product, would you believe him? Why or why not? Why are we so skeptical of the word *true* today? Then read **verses 16–27** and begin your study of Scripture.

Searching the Scriptures

Temptations Offer Only the Best

1. The first part of this lesson, **verses 16–18,** serves as a continuation of James' statement about temptation **(vv. 13–15).**

Adam and Eve might have said they were only trying to "better" themselves—seeking knowledge of good and evil.

2–4. In considering the temptation of Jesus, as well as His ministry in general, it is important to keep in mind that Holy Scripture and the Creeds distinguish but never separate the two natures of Jesus Christ, as if He acted first according to one nature, and then the other. Jesus Christ is one Person, true God and true man. Jesus used God's Word to overcome temptation. Jesus depended on that which was true, right, and unchanging—God's Word. We too can rely completely upon the power of the Holy Spirit working through God's Word to enable us to withstand and overcome temptations.

"I Believe …"

1. The name "Father" suggests a personal relationship. In the Apostles' Creed, the word "Father" expresses the redeemed relationship between God and us through Jesus Christ by the work of the Holy Spirit. Accordingly, James' statement in **verse 17** and the name "Father" in the First Article of the Creed do not refer to a "first cause" or a vague "God out there" who

can be known through natural instinct or natural religion. This is the Father of our Lord Jesus Christ and our Father, who has created us, and who through Christ's death and resurrection has reconciled us to Himself. He is the Giver of "every good and perfect gift" **(v. 17)**.

2–4. The "Father of heavenly lights, who does not change like shifting shadows" **(v. 17)** is the God whom we know by faith in Christ. He "chose to give us birth through the word of truth" **(v. 18),** that is, He has called, enlightened, and sanctified us to be His children. (Luther, Small Catechism, explanation of the Third Article.)

Born to Live

1. In **verse 18** birth is compared to redemption, contrasting it to death in **verse 15.** The phrase "every good and perfect gift is from above" in **verse 17** helps to explain that the Father "chose" **(v. 18)** that we be spiritually reborn. See **1 Peter 1:23.**

2. Christians are "firstfruits" of Christ's death and resurrection because we live our new life in Him. Sharing in Christ's death and resurrection, we are born anew. Our faith and life in Christ are the fruit of His resurrection victory.

3. The Holy Spirit brings us to faith in Jesus Christ **(1 Cor. 12:3; John 3:5–6).** The Holy Spirit through the Law convicts us of our sinfulness **(John 16:8–9).** He also teaches us the words of God and of Christ, so that we believe and trust in God for life and salvation **(John 14:16, 26; 16:13–14; Acts 2:4–11; 4:8–12).**

Listening and Doing

1–2. Truly listening to another person is the key to good communication skills. By listening to others we indicate that we value their ideas and input and care about their feelings. This reaffirms their personal value.

3–4. There are two thoughts regarding anger in **verse 20.** First, people who are full of sinful anger do not practice the kind of conduct that is just and right in God's eyes. Anger and other sins are companions—one often leads to the other. Second, when God's servants display sinful anger and the passions that go with it, their negative witness makes it harder for nonbelievers to lay hold of the truth that God is moral and just and always does what is right.

"In One Ear …" Why Not?

1–3. We are tempted to hear—not do. We can easily deceive ourselves into doing nothing. In view of the imagery of birth in **verse 15** (sin and death) and **verse 18** (grace and life), we might say that the negative phrase "do not merely listen to the word, and so deceive yourselves" (**v. 22**) suggests no birth at all. Nothing happens. Actually, to be a hearer only is the dead "fruit" of wavering, or unbelief. That fruitlessness is the opposite of the fruitfulness of God's implanted Word (**v. 21;** see also **Matt. 7:26**).

4. Each of the phrases suggest the fruitfulness of God's Word of truth, the implanted word (**v. 21**). God keeps His promises. He fulfills them in blessing. That is also a part of the meaning of "firstfruits" (**v. 18**).

Motivated by the Gospel

1–3. The Law convicts us of our sinfulness—the Gospel proclaims forgiveness and a new life through Christ's death and resurrection. Since the Law condemns rather than gives life, since it points out our captivity to Satan, it cannot give us liberty. The Law itself destroys, rather than creates.

In the Old Testament, the word "torah" (law)—depending on the context—at times means the entire Word of God (judgment and promise, e.g., **Ps. 119:97**) and not just judgment only. The word was familiar to Jewish Christians. James uses the word "law" in the phrase "perfect law that gives freedom" (**v. 25**) figuratively. Actually James is talking about the Gospel of Christ, which gives us liberty from the guilt and slavery of sin and the liberty in His name to forgive and serve as we have been forgiven and served (**John 8:34–36**).

"Pure" and "faultless" religion are demonstrated by those who have received "the crown of life" through faith in Christ Jesus. We are not skeptical of these words because we have experienced the promises of God and know them to be true.

The Word for Us

Allow time for participants to share insights they have learned from this study as they discuss the questions in this section.

Closing

Sing or speak together stanzas 1, 3, and 5 of "O God of Mercy, God of Light."

Lesson 5
From Partiality to Servanthood
(James 2:1–13)

Before the Session

Study carefully **James 2:1–13.** Review the study guide materials in conjunction with the leaders notes. Be attune to newspaper articles or television shows that might provide you with examples of prejudice.

The Class Session

Ask a volunteer to begin the class with prayer. Read aloud the "Theme Verse," "Goal," and "What's Going On Here?" from the study guide. Use the first two questions under "Searching the Scriptures" to begin a discussion on prejudice. Share examples of prejudice and partiality that you have observed this past week to get the discussion rolling.

Searching the Scriptures

Partial? Who, Me?

1–2. Other words for partiality are "prejudice," "discrimination," and "favoritism." Nepotism and cronyism are specific kinds of partiality. Use these questions to help participants recognize partiality and prejudice in themselves, in their community, and in their congregation.

3–5. Partiality goes hand in hand with being judgmental. It is also interesting to note that whenever we are partial to another person we are probably more patient with that person (for the wrong reasons) than with others. That again is being judgmental.

James' warning about partiality and injustice might well have called to the mind of Jewish Christians Old Testament passages such as the following: **Lev. 19:15; Deut. 1:17; 10:1, 7–19; 16:19–20.** Although there are only five quotations from the Old Testament in the epistle of James, there are many indirect references like the above passages. The five quotations and some of their Old Testament background are **James 1:11—Is. 40:6–7; 2:8—Lev. 19:18; 2:11—Ex. 20:13; 2:23—Gen. 15:6; 4:6—Prov. 3:34.**

There's Always a Reason

1. We have to confess that we can often find a reason to explain our partialities. Each reason is a self-justifying one.

When it comes to partiality, one person's "freedom" is another person's loss. Thus we have the partiality toward the rich at the expense of the poor, and to the powerful at the expense of the weak, to the well-dressed at the expense of the poorly dressed **(2:2–3)**. These distinctions are judgments with evil thoughts **(2:4)**.

2. The double-minded person referred to in **verse 8** is one who wavers back and forth between faith and the world. It describes one who is tempted by all the world has to offer, its lusts and values. Thus, the double-minded person may fall easy prey to partiality and prejudice if they serve to better him or make him more comfortable. Our faith life requires single-mindedness: by the Holy Spirit working through God's Word to strengthen our faith we can remain tuned in to the Lord and His ways, which do not allow for prejudice.

3. Note the contrast between this exercise of power and the servanthood that James referred to in his greeting to his brothers in the faith **(1:2)**. It is only the child of God who can receive power from the Holy Spirit to treat people with loving impartiality.

Rich in Faith

1. Let participants discuss this question and give examples from their lives.

2. The economically poor are often, but not always, more open to God and the riches of His grace **(2:5)**. Having little in life, they may be all the more aware of their dependence on God. Wealth as such may not necessarily be a tempting idol to them (see **Mark 10:25**). Bitterness against God and other people may be more of a direct temptation for poor people.

Here Comes the Judge

1. To the eyes of the world, the Christian poor may seem to be easy victims for two reasons. One, they do not have the financial resources to fight back (cf. **2:6**). Two, like any other Christian they should not manipulate and victimize others (cf. **Matt. 7:12**).

2. It is necessary for the legal system to protect one person or organization from others. But legality does not always determine morality. Laws can be used to liberate, but also to control and to bind. Laws and court pronouncements can be legal—but still wrong or oppressive (e.g., on abortion).

The Sting of the Law

1. Partiality to one's neighbor is a transgression of the Law, even though our preference of one person over another because of his riches or position may seem ever so slight.

2. Allow participants to share examples of how partiality breaks the

commandments, for example, we break the Eighth Commandment when we show partiality or prejudice because we are not defending our neighbor against wrongdoing or helping him maintain his rights.

3. If at any one time we think that we are not breaking one law (a deception), we are at the same time faced with our obvious breaking of another. One may say, for example, that he does not commit adultery (outwardly at least), but in his partiality (harm) against his neighbor he breaks the Fifth Commandment, and in effect thereby the whole Law **(2:10–11)**, and stands condemned.

The Servanthood of Royalty

1–2. Loving neighbor as self is "royal" because it is a sovereign summary of the whole Law. The phrase "law that gives freedom" **(2:12)** means more than just the Ten Commandments. It refers specifically to the Gospel, whereby God the Father declares us forgiven for the sake of Christ, our King, who fulfilled the Law for us.

3. Jesus Christ fulfilled the Law by keeping it in our stead. He "fulfilled" the Law also by suffering and dying in our place—death is the ultimate sting of the Law (i.e., the death that comes from sin, **1:15**). By His resurrection, Jesus gives us the kingly victory of His servanthood to us, and through our ministry of Word and Sacraments to others (see **1 Peter 2:9**). In the power of His forgiveness we are freed to keep the Law—not in order to earn salvation, but because we are already saved.

4. Allow participants time to discuss this question and offer examples. Remind them that when we too fail to be merciful we turn in repentance to our Lord, who has promised to forgive us. His love for us in Christ Jesus empowers us to live for Him.

The Word for Us

As you have time, bring your discussion of prejudice and partiality together in your closing discussion. Emphasize the positive contribution that Christians can make toward overcoming prejudice. Talk about how we can repent of our prejudice and try to come up with specific suggestions for dealing more lovingly with people in our own homes and families.

Closing

Sing or speak together stanzas 4 and 5 of "O Fount of Good, for All Your Love." Conclude with a prayer that includes concerns of the participants.

Lesson 6

The Fruitfulness of Faith in Christ
(James 2:14–26)

Before the Session

Pray that the Holy Spirit will bless your study time by leading you into a deeper understanding of the relationship between faith and works. Then read **James 2:14–26** and read the study guide and leaders notes.

The Class Session

Begin with prayer. Ask a volunteer to read the "Theme Verse," "Goal," and "What's Going On Here?" from the study guide. Then do the following introductory exercise. Give each participant a piece of paper. Then write these questions on the board one at a time:

1. Whom do you trust?
2. Whom do you trust with your life?
3. What is salvation?
4. How are you saved?

Ask each to write a brief answer. Then share your answers. How might the answers be different if the members of the class were non-Christian?

Then look for Jesus' answers to these questions in **James 1:1, 12, 18** and **2:1, 5.**

For clear Christian proclamation, it is important to specify that Christian "faith" is faith in Christ, in the triune God.

Is Dead Faith Still "Faith"?

1–4. Faith and works cannot be separated, as if a person can have a choice about how he wants to be saved, by either faith or works **(2:18).** Faith in Christ does not exist in a vacuum. Faith without works is a contradiction. Faith in Christ always produces fruit. God's Word always accomplishes its purpose **(Is. 55:11).**

5. James' own example is quite pointed **(2:14–18).** It is an example that is at once universal, realistic, and contemporary. There is no profit at all in saying words, even "religious words," but then not providing help. James says **(2:14–17)** that ministry to the soul cannot be separated from ministry to the body. If a person looks to this life only, he will lose it **(Matt. 6:24; 10:39; 16:26).** And ministry is always ministry to the whole person and not just to selected needs we think we can fulfill.

Actions Speak Louder Than Words

1–2. Discuss the examples. You might add these from **James: 1:6, 23, and 2:8–9.** Other examples from Scripture are **Hos. 8:1–4; Matt. 7:21; 23:14, 23; 25:11–12; Luke 6:46; 13:25.** If you wish, this discussion section can be used at the end of the lesson in conjunction with the items under "The Word for Us."

Head Knowledge Only

1. James' charge to his hearers about believing there is only one God **(2:19)** may be an attempt to remind them of the great creed and confession of Judaism, the Shema (hear): "Hear, O Israel: The LORD our God, the LORD is one" **(Deut. 6:4).** (See **Deut. 6:4–9; 11:13–21; Num. 15:37–41.**) The words make the judgment all the more pointed for any Jewish Christians who might claim to have faith without living it.

2. In comparing the parable of the fig tree and these verses of James, discuss the statement of Law or accusation both contain and how they drive us to the Gospel of forgiveness, for none of us perfectly live our faith nor perfectly produce fruits of faith.

3. In **Gal. 5:6** Paul notes that the only thing that counts is faith expressing itself through acts of love. Faith is not head knowledge only, but a living and active trust in Jesus as Savior that expresses itself in love for God by loving acts towards others.

Are You a Classic Example?

1–2. Paul also referred to Abraham as a classic example of faith. There is no contradiction between James and Paul. Paul emphasized that Abraham was saved by faith in God, not by works separate from faith **(Rom. 4:3, 9, 22; Gal. 3:6).** James emphasized that Abraham's "faith [in God] and his actions were working together" **(2:22).** Abraham's works were the fruits of his trust in God. In that sense, James also says that Abraham's "faith was made complete by what he did" **(2:22).** We confess that we are saved by God's grace through faith in Christ, without good works as a cause or an aid (the doctrine of justification). We also say with equal emphasis and insistence (as do James, Paul, and Jesus) that faith in Christ is evident and shown in its fullness by the fruits of faith (the doctrine of sanctification).

The correct understanding of the relationship between justification and sanctification is vital in the Christian life. On the one hand, if we think we must earn our way, do good and work to gain some place in the salvation plan of God, we nullify the work of Christ and place ourselves in desperate trouble. On the other hand, if we try to keep faith as some kind of reserve insurance policy against death and hell, we distort the Gospel, make Christian life and service meaningless, and pretend at believing. In either case the gracious plan of God for our salvation is spurned.

3. James and Paul agree in their theology. The problems they deal with are different. Paul maintains that a person is not saved by good works (**Rom. 3:28; Eph. 2:8–9**). James agrees. James emphasizes that this saving faith in Christ is fruitful, and that where there is faith in Christ, there are good works, the fruits of faith. Paul agrees.

4. Discuss questions based on information from the Bible references.

The Word for Us

1-2. Use the people mentioned in Hebrews and James to discuss the meaning of the faith/works relationship in our Christian life.

3. Help participants apply what they've learned by reviewing the statements under "Actions Speak Louder Than Words" in this lesson. Try to come up with specific suggestions and encouragement for the faith-life of your participants and your congregation.

Closing

Ask participants for prayer requests. Then have them close in silent prayer, incorporating the thoughts from the "Closing" section of the study guide and any prayer requests mentioned. Or lead the closing prayer yourself.

Lesson 7
A Treacherous Tongue (James 3:1–12)

Before the Session

Read **James 3:1–12** and your study materials. Ask God to bless your preparation.

The Class Session

Open with prayer. Ask for a volunteer to read the "Theme Verse," "Goal," and "What's Going On Here?" from the study guide. If you have 10 or more people in your group and you can spread out a little, try this experiment to test the tongue's reliability. Tell a brief account of some news item to the person next to you. (E.g., two cars hit head-on route 43, just past highway Z. One was going west at a high rate of speed, crossed the center line, and struck a second car. The driver of the first car was drunk. He was injured. His passenger was killed, and four people in the other car were hospitalized.) Ask each person in turn to tell the story to his neighbor. Then check the accuracy of the last account.

Why was the account so inaccurate? Is our tongue that unreliable? What does that say about us?

Searching the Scriptures

For the Teacher

1. Other than an example, the reason for James' singling out teachers is not clear. James might have been referring to self-styled teachers who spoke in the synagogues as they passed through the villages. They, like Jesus and His disciples, had access to the synagogues (**Matt. 12:9; 13:54; Mark 1:39**), although they were not always invited back (**Luke 4:28–29**).

2. More is expected of teachers. The judgment on the careless shepherds of Israel is harsh, as recorded for example in **Ezek. 34:1–19.** Scripture speaks of judgment beginning at home (**1 Peter 4:17; cf. Matt. 7:15**). Also, Paul expressed personal concern so that he himself after having preached the Gospel would not be disqualified (**1 Cor. 9:27**).

3. The basic corruption of humankind, following the fall into sin (**Gen. 3:6–7**) displays itself in every way. Luther characteristically emphasized the sinfulness of humankind, rather than just a list of actual sins. It is that original sinfulness which the tongue betrays.

Summarizing Article I of the Formula of Concord: Man is not created evil or corrupt. God does not create evil. Therefore nature is not sinful. But following the fall into sin, man's nature is corrupted and sinful. In that sense we say we "are by nature sinful and unclean." The tongue is not only a culprit, but also a witness against us.

Imagery: The Language of Pictures

1–2. James often uses picture language (imagery) to make his points, and he draws much of his figurative language from nature and animals. Like Jesus' parables he uses the familiar to teach. See **Matt. 6:26; 7:9–10; 8:20.**

The Terrible Tongue

1–2. Here the judgment is expressed effectively; **verses 5–12** are a sharp statement of the Law. The tongue is the focus.

It is ironic that the tongue, which seems to be small and subservient, has so much power. To our shame our small tongue controls us in heart and mind and body. The tongue is uncontrollable; it is indeed "a restless evil, full of deadly poison" **(3:8).**

Hell's Representative

1–3. Discuss the way in which the tongue is involved in all of our sinfulness: anger, **1:19–20;** temptation, **1:14–15;** and faith that does not come alive in the Christian, **2:14–17.** In each case the tongue betrays the inner heart. It reveals the anger or fraud we try to live. Its very activity accuses and condemns us. Relate its accusation to **Matt. 12:36–37.**

4. The Greek word for "hell" in **3:6** is *gehenna;* like *hades* it is one of the words translated as "hell" in the New Testament. *Gehenna* is the Greek word for the Hebrew *Hinnom.* The Hinnom Valley is south and southwest of Jerusalem. It had been a place of inhuman, idolatrous practices. In Scripture, the Valley of Hinnom or Gehenna was considered an unclean, horrible place—a place of detestation, evil, and judgment. It became an expression of God's judgment. Other references, for example, are **2 Chron. 28:3; Jer. 7:31–33; Matt. 5:22.** "Set on fire by hell" **(3:6)** would be clear to Jewish Christians.

Wanted: A Tongue Tamer

1–2. If people cannot tame the tongue, let alone root out its evil, then it is particularly evident that man cannot save himself. Only Jesus Christ spoke no evil. The charges of blasphemy were false **(Matt. 27:4, 23–24).** There was no guile in Him **(1 Peter 2:22).** He was hanged on a tree for us **(Acts 5:30).**

The underlying irony and judgment are expressed in **3:7–8.** Man can tame every kind of beast, but he cannot tame his own tongue! The tongue is a "restless" evil. "Restless" carefully describes the evil that darts about, eager and ill at ease unless it is doing further evil. No wonder James also says that the tongue is full of deadly poison and that no human being can tame it **(3:8).** Only through faith strengthened by the power of the Holy Spirit working through God's Word can the tongue be tamed.

A Paradox

1–2. But now the contradiction (and a further irony): We who have received the promise of God by faith in Christ, we who have received the righteousness of God as a gracious gift, find ourselves "double-tongued" (fork-tongued?). With the tongue we bless the Lord and Father. With it we also curse our fellowmen, who are made in the likeness of God **(3:9),** that is holy and without sin (see **Gen. 1:26–27; Col. 3:10; Eph. 4:24).** From the same mouth comes blessing and cursing. James' comment on that is really an understatement: "My brothers, this should not be" **(3:10).** The tongue reveals our self most clearly. We are sinner and saint. And we would destroy ourselves were it not for the continued grace and forgiveness we are given in Jesus Christ. Only the tree—cross—on which Jesus suffered and died permits us to bear the fruit of faith through our tongues—what we say and do.

3. Knowing that God for Jesus' sake forgives penitent sinners gives us comfort since we know God will forgive us when we come to Him in repentance for the troubles our tongues have caused.

The Word for Us

Allow participants to read, reflect upon, and make an action plan for the suggestions in this section of the study guide. Encourage participants to work on these.

Closing

Speak or sing stanzas 1 and 3 of "Take My Life, O Lord, Renew."

Lesson 8
The Wisdom of Faith (James 3:13–18)

Before the Session

Read **James 3:13–18** along with these notes. Check out the introduction of a few Bible commentaries on wisdom literature (e.g., a commentary on Proverbs) to gain a better understanding of the biblical view of wisdom.

The Class Session

Begin your class with prayer. Ask someone to read the "Theme Verse," "Goal," and "What's Going On Here?" from the study guide. Then write the words "wisdom" and "wise" on the board. Ask for definitions. Write some of them down. Leave them so that the class can see them as you discuss. Return to your list at the end of the class session in your discussion of "The Word for Us."

Searching the Scriptures

The Unwisdom of the Wise

1. Read **James 3:13–18**. Then begin discussing the material. Ask for

specific examples of the way in which we show our own foolishness even as we try to be wise. You need not spend a lot of time on this, but the discussion should help personalize the strong statement of Law in this portion of James and help the participants realize how incomplete our own wisdom is, how faulty our understanding, when compared to God's ideal, and how much we need God's wisdom.

2. Examples from Scripture that reflect inconsistencies (or the difference between the wisdom of trust in God and the worldly "wisdom" of evil) are Saul's saving animals from the spoils of war for a sacrifice **(1 Sam. 15)**; David's giving Uriah a furlough to attempt a cover-up of his own adultery **(2 Sam. 11:6–13)**; the Pharisee and publican in the temple **(Luke 18:10–14)**; the disciples rebuking those who brought little children to Jesus **(Luke 18:15–17)**.

Other Examples (Besides You)

1–2. In light of **2:21–23** and **3:13** Abraham appears wise and understanding. His life showed works of faith in the "humility that comes from wisdom." (Yet, lest we falsely idealize Abraham, we might remember that he was not always wise either. In **Gen. 12:10–20,** e.g., Abraham told a half truth, or lie, when for fear of his life he called his wife, a half sister, his sister.) God had promised Abraham and Sarah a child after they were too old ordinarily to have children **(Gen. 17:17).** Sarah miraculously had a son. Later Abraham was told to sacrifice that son—the son of the promise. In terms of human understanding, that command would hardly be called "wisdom." Yet Abraham believed God. Troubled in soul, he trusted God, and obeyed. That is the wisdom of faith in God, the wisdom "that comes from heaven" **(3:17).**

3. It may have seemed that Rahab was unwise in hiding the "enemy" and collaborating with them. She might even have been accused of being an opportunist who exercised the worldly "wisdom" of selfish gain. But, on the basis of Scriptural testimony, her motives were evidently quite different. They were the motives of trust in God, of the wisdom of faith **(2:25).**

James' encouragement to be wise and understanding continues a long-standing appeal in God's Word. In **Deut. 4:5–6,** for example, we have Moses' exhortation to Israel to live truthfully according to God's Word. If the Israelites would follow God and His Word, then, after they entered the Promised Land, they would be known as a great nation, as "a wise and understanding people." (For other passages on wisdom, see **Job 28:28; Ps. 111:10; Prov. 9:10; Is. 5:21; Matt. 5:16; 1 Cor. 1:18–2:13; 1 Peter 2:12.**)

4. Accept examples from class members. Underscore that God's people

act out of wisdom when they act in agreement with His design revealed in His Word.

Wisdom from Below

1. James' description of the unwise is in substance and character the same that Paul gives when he lists the works of the Law in **Gal. 5:19–21.** The Greek word translated "selfish ambition" **(James 3:14)** can also be translated as "strife" or "contention." It is derived from the word *hireling*, which is characterized by partisanship (cf. "favoritism" of **2:9**) and a factious spirit.

2–4. All boasting is tainted with lying if it is not outright lying (no essential difference), because what a person boasts of is idolatrous and selfish **(3:16).** The only legitimate "boasting" is that of thankful trust for God's grace through Jesus Christ (see **1:18**). Finally, we can determine the person with real God-given wisdom the same way Jesus told us to test the false teachers in **Matt. 7:15–20,** by what that wisdom or teacher produces.

Wisdom from Above

1–6. Go through each of the virtues of wisdom. As you discuss each, see if you can relate the ideal to your own life. How are we pure, open-minded, gentle, and the like? What makes us fail to be those things? It is the wisdom of faith in Christ to be peaceable, gentle, merciful. It literally takes faith in Christ to be a peacemaker, for it means that one is like a lamb before the wolves **(Luke 10:3),** exposed to be taken advantage of. The Lord asks us not to fight, not shrewdly to manipulate others, but to do good to others. We are even to love our enemies and not to curse them **(2:8–10; Matt. 5:44).**

The Word for Us

1–3. We never attain perfect wisdom, because in this life on earth we are yet sinners; we Christians still struggle against our old sinful selves. Like Paul, we daily have to confess that we do what we do not want to do **(Rom. 7:21–8:1).** Our sinfulness struggles against our redeemed, liberated life in Christ. This is what Luther calls the sinner/saint paradox. We are sinners, yet at the same time saints because of Christ's death and resurrection for us. God does promise to strengthen and preserve our faith through His Word. Therefore, Bible study, worship, and personal devotions should be included on a practical "to do" list.

Thus Paul can also write that it is no longer he who lives but Christ who lives in him **(Gal. 2:20;** see also **Col. 3:10; Phil. 4:13).** True wisdom is a gift—and our wisdom is our faith in Jesus Christ as Savior.

Closing

Sing or speak together "I Pray You, Dear Lord Jesus" as your closing prayer.

Lesson 9

Love of the World and Love of God
(James 4:1–10)

Before the Session

Read **James 4:1–10** along with a good commentary. Pray for the individuals in your class and ask God to bless your preparation.

The Class Session

Begin with prayer. Have someone read the "Theme Verse," "Goal," and "What's Going On Here?" sections. If possible show some pictures of war. Ask members of the class to recount some of their experiences with war either as a participant or an observer. Don't force personal revelation but try to share some of the individual horror that war is. Then ask: Is war really necessary? Is it inevitable? Why? Then read the first paragraph of "Searching the Scriptures" and begin your study of the text.

Searching the Scriptures

Seen Any Good Wars Lately?

1. James develops an image to show the danger and destructiveness of fighting and conflict. You might talk about conflict and the way in which Christians can solve their conflicts. (See also **Rom. 7:23; 1 Peter 2:11.**)

2. The word translated as "want" or "desire" (in some translations) in **4:2** has the same meaning in **1:14–15.** In **1 Peter 1:12** ("long") it is used in a good sense. (Cf. **1 Peter 2:2.**)

3. Allow participants to discuss.

4. James is pointing out what can and does happen when people seek to satisfy their own sinful desires to the exclusion of God's good for them. Consider various biblical and historical examples. For instance, the obvious example of David's coveting Uriah's wife, Bathsheba, and thus arranging for Uriah's murder in order to have her.

Mirror, Mirror on the Wall

1. We are convicted in our self-centered idolatry by James' straightforward accusations. The Fifth Commandment (kill) and the Ninth and Tenth Commandments (coveting) are given direct expression. The Fourth (dishonor), Seventh (stealing, plundering), and Eighth (speaking evil) are involved. Even the Sixth (abuse of sex, personhood) is involved. Our whole relationship to our "neighbor" is accused. And finally we are convicted of the whole Law, for our misuse of our neighbor stems from our sinful pride—the worship of ourselves and the breaking of the First Commandment—and surely the Second and Third Commandments as well (God's name and worship).

2. If a person does not ask God, in effect he depends on himself and draws from his own desires and passions. He reaps what he has sown **(Gal. 6:7).** He gets what he asks for; (because of his bondage to the corruption of sin) he ends up getting nothing **(Job 4:8; Phil. 3:19).**

We "ask with wrong motives" (1) when we seek satisfaction for our own sinful desires (passions) and (2) when our motives and purpose are wrong. We struggle, only to have things end up with corruption, evil, and death **(Rom. 6:23; 2 Peter 2:12).**

3. "No one can serve two masters. ... he will be devoted to the one and despise the other," says Jesus **(Matt. 6:24).** The First Commandment indicates that God wants our total allegiance, "You shall have no other gods before Me." When God is first in our life, everything else falls into its rightful place. We are free to serve Him and enjoy the blessings He gives without being controlled by them.

God's Heartache

1. There are two schools of thought on to whom or what James is referring in **James 4:5.** The first maintains that it is the Holy Spirit (see **1 Sam. 16:13; Rom. 15:13**) who jealously wants our devotion (**Ex. 20:5**). The second says "the spirit he caused to live in us" refers to God's creation of man (see **Gen. 2:7**). Because of the fall, humankind's spirit envies intensely and is prone to fighting. This interpretation makes sense when followed by **verse 6,** which counters that God's grace is stronger. It is able to overcome man's envy. Moreover, His grace is a free gift to us!

2. James' appeal is to the grace of God brought by the Holy Spirit. It is his basic message (see **1:5, 18, 21,** etc.). Since James all along has been addressing Christians, even though he severely condemns, it is "natural" that he would speak of God's patient mercy and love, His willingness to forgive the repentant, to give "more grace" **(4:6).** The phrase "more grace" reminds one of Paul's statement in **Rom. 5:20:** "Where sin increased, grace

increased all the more." (See also **1 Tim. 1:14–15.**) The passages indicate how God responds to our need for His forgiveness.

3. For source and parallel passages to the quotation "God opposes the proud but gives grace to the humble" **(4:6)** see **Prov. 3:34–35; Ps. 138:6; Is. 57:15; Matt. 23:11–12; 1 Peter 5:5.**

Draw Near to God

1. The promise should be emphasized. "To resist the devil" means to trust in God. He has overcome Satan for us **(John 12:31; 16:11; Matt. 12:28; Luke 10:18–20).**

2. You could discuss the strong connection with the Old Testament in these verses and in the entire epistle. James sounds very much like an Old Testament prophet in form and style. His Hebrew hearers would have recognized his message as a clear call to repentance similar to the call of Hosea, Amos, Jeremiah, and many others.

3. The humble are those who acknowledge their status as God's creatures, recognize their insufficiency apart from Christ, and desire fellowship with God in Jesus Christ. The admonition and promise in **verse 9** are a parallel to that in **verse 7:** "Resist the devil, and he will flee from you." The appeal "to humble" oneself means to repent of one's sinfulness. It is understood that our trust is to be in Jesus Christ's death and resurrection for our forgiveness and reconciliation. That is our exaltation. God lifts us up to be His own. Then our sorrow is turned to joy **(Is. 51:11).** A parallel passage to **4:10** is **1 Peter 5:5–6.**

Exalting us, the Holy Spirit brings to fruitful completion God's jealous yearning **(4:5)** by dwelling and working within us the victory of Christ's resurrection.

The Word for Us

1–2. To clarify the use of the Law, talk about the relevance and effectiveness of James' words today. We come with other backgrounds and expectations than did the Hebrews who first read James. Center on the purpose of this prophetic exposition of Law—to bring us to the knowledge of our sin and point us to the cross of Christ for forgiveness and renewal.

3. Help participants put what they have learned in this lesson into practice. Remind them that our relationship with each other can only be restored through the power of the Holy Spirit working through the Gospel.

Closing

Sing or speak stanzas 1 and 3 of "God of Grace and God of Glory" as your closing prayer.

Lesson 10
What Is Your Life? (James 4:11–17)

Before the Session
Study **James 4:11–17** and the study guide material along with a good commentary. Pray that God will bless your preparations.

The Class Session
Ask a volunteer to open with prayer. Have another person read the "Theme Verse," "Goal," and "What's Going On Here?" from the study guide. Then write the words *Brother (Sister)* and *Friend* on the board. Ask the class to list ways the words are the same. How are they different? What does it say about God when we say we are brothers? In what way is Jesus our brother? Move into "Searching the Scriptures."

Invite volunteers to read aloud **James 4:11–17.**

Searching the Scriptures
Brother
1–2. In **4:11**, James leads in an interesting way into his point about not judging another. James typically addresses his hearers as "brothers," and here, additionally, he admonishes them not to be unbrotherly by speaking evil against or judging another brother.

The word "brother" suggests a relationship of respect, concern, and love. James' address to his hearers as "dear brothers" **(1:16)** is an acknowledgement of their oneness in the body of Christ, the holy Christian church. It is contradictory as well as unchristian, therefore, for a brother not to treat a brother as a "brother." It is unneighborly not to act as a "neighbor" to one's neighbor.

A Judge! Who, Me?
1. Building on the concept of brotherhood it is a contradiction to judge (condemn) a brother. The reasoning in **4:11** is something like this:

Any brother who speaks evil against another brother breaks the brotherhood, and ignores the law that forbids attacking a brother.

In ignoring the law a person declares the law to be a bad law, which is the same as judging the law.

When a person judges the law to be no good, he declares the lawgiver (God) also to be deficient.

2. In that line of reasoning the question in **4:12** "Who are you … ?" is an

effective "put-down," especially since it follows his direct statement that there is only one Lawgiver and Judge. Again we stand condemned. We should handle our brother in love, ready and eager to forgive his faults.

3. There is quite a contrast between (1) God's love and desire to redeem and save all humankind, and (2) our judging one another (and the Law) by speaking evil against each other. Compare the way we ordinarily act **(4:12b)** with the way we are told to deal with our brother **(2:12–13)**.

Let's Make Some Money!

1–4. James' reference to commercial travel suggests the dispersion of the Jews—some of them having become Christians. Dispersed from their homeland, many of the Jews congregated in the cities and engaged in commerce.

James points out that we humans "do not even know what will happen tomorrow" **(4:14)**. To talk as if we do is to boast in our arrogance **(4:16)**. That is empty talk, foolish talk. James says that "All such boasting is evil." Who are we to say what life is and how long it lasts? For life is like a vapor or mist that appears momentarily and disappears **(4:14)**. You might also point out the picture of life as fleeting in **1:10–11**. To plan arrogantly for the future is foolish. Our soul might be required. Although James does not condemn making money or gaining a profit, he does warn his listeners to remember that which is most important—our faith in Christ Jesus. James warns against anything that would cause us to no longer fear and trust in God above all things.

If It Is the Lord's Will

1–2. "If it is the Lord's will" is a statement of trust. The word "if" in the English translation is not to be considered as an expression of doubt. We put ourselves into God's gracious, forgiving care and keeping. We plan ahead, make schedules, prepare carefully, but we place all our life and activities into the hands of the Lord. We trust God (not the world or ourselves) for the welfare of our lives and our future.

By turning **verse 17** of **chapter 4** around into a positive statement, we are reminded of James' earlier statement in **1:25**: "the man … doing it—he will be blessed in what he does." And that leads us also to the blessing and the promise as given in **3:17**.

The Word for Us

1–2. In **4:13–16,** James is not condemning good management and planning for the future. The good stewards in **Matt. 25:14–21,** for example, who increased the money their master gave them, planned carefully. They lived and worked expectantly in anticipation of their master's return. Their profitable handling of the money was a fruit of their faithfulness to their master. A Christian lives in anticipation of Christ's final coming. By being faithful in his daily work he is always ready.

Try to come up with specific ways in which God can be included in our personal, family, and congregational planning. Write all the suggestions down. Perhaps you can share the participants' list by means of a poster or note in the newsletter or bulletin.

3. James' reference here to sins of omission—knowing what we ought to do, but failing to do it—reflects Jesus' teaching in many of His parables. For example, in the parable of the talents **(Matt. 25:14–30)** Jesus emphasizes using the gifts He has given for Kingdom work. In the parable about the sheep and goats at the final judgment **(Matt. 25:31–46)** Jesus' emphasis is not on the various sinful acts unbelievers have committed and believers have not. Rather, He commends those who have shown mercy and love to their fellow human beings, and in doing so, have shown love to Him. We who believe in Christ need to constantly examine ourselves not only for sins we do commit but for failing to do the good we know we should.

As sinners we come to our Lord in repentance for our lack of love and service and seek the empowering of the Holy Spirit to live for Jesus. The Good News is that God loves, forgives, and equips us for His Kingdom work through faith in Christ Jesus.

Closing

Close by praying the prayer in the study guide.

Lesson 11
The Love of Money (James 5:1–6)

Before the Session

Pray that the Holy Spirit will lead you into a deeper understanding of God's Word. Take the concerns of the participants in your class before the Lord in prayer. Read **James 5:1–6**, the study guide, and leaders notes along with a good commentary.

The Class Session

Begin with prayer. Ask someone to read the "Theme Verse," "Goal," and "What's Going On Here?" from the study guide. Read **James 5:1–6** and begin your work on the text.

Searching the Scriptures

How Now

1. Since this portion is probably addressed to Christians who let riches get in the way of their faith-life, it speaks a word of Law to us. Examples of judgment in **5:1–6** are the following: weeping and wailing because of the miseries to come (**v. 1**); the rotten riches and moth-eaten clothing (**v. 2**); rust, devoured flesh, and fire (**v. 3**); and the Lord hearing the cries of the poor (**v. 4**). The tone of judgment strongly suggests that the situation will soon be reversed, so that the rich will be condemned (see **Prov. 3:32–35**).

2. Almost all of the judgments are a part of the final judgment. Phrases that imply the last judgment are "the last days," "testify against you," and "like fire" in **verse 3**. Those are said to be "coming upon you" in **verse 1**.

3. The rich are deceived in their security in riches since their gold and silver are corroded (**v. 3**). Ironically, they have "fattened themselves" on wealth and material possessions, thus making themselves ready for "the day of slaughter" (**v. 5**). They have a false sense of security because they seem to get their own way (**v. 6**) but judgment awaits them (**v. 1**).

You might discuss recent events that show the emptiness and self-deception of wealth. The point would not simply be to find fault but to see the truth of these judgments as they apply also to us. Your discussion will lead into the next part.

How Are You Doing?

1–2. This discussion should be personal but not threatening. No one needs to reveal private sins. Neither should it be just a gripe session about others' faults. The discussion should lead to repentance and a pronouncement of God's declaration of grace.

Self-Deception and Judgment

1. Clothing was one of the main forms of wealth in biblical times. "Rotted" and "eaten" can refer to both what is already happening (the rich would rather their wealth be eaten up and spoiled than share it with others) as well as the final result of all material possessions at the end time. Moreover, at the final judgment the wealth of the rich will no longer be an asset but will become a judgment against them.

2. Since silver and gold do not corrode or rust, the point is simply that they are perishable. Like every physical thing they cannot last forever.

3. The word "wealth" expresses the self-centered idolatry of a person who delights and trusts in his riches. Using the Matthew reference, talk about the need for our investment of ourselves and our attention in heavenly things. How do we get the strength to do that? Remind participants that the Holy Spirit strengthens our faith through God's Word enabling us to invest our energy in heavenly things.

Champion of the Oppressed

1–2. In James' imagery and statements of judgment as expressed in **5:2–4,** there is a dual movement toward a climax: (1) from things to people, and (2) from moth and corrosion (which bring nothing) to God Himself as the One who will bring the false treasures of the rich to nothing.

Other passages in Scripture about the judgment on withheld wages are **Lev. 19:13; Mal. 3:5.** See also **Luke 10:7.**

For other examples of the Lord's hearing the cry of the oppressed, see **Gen. 4:10** (Abel's blood), **Gen. 18:20; 19:13** (wickedness in Sodom), **Ex. 3:7** (enslaved Israel in Egypt), and **Ps. 18:6** (a believer's prayer for help).

3. **Verse 6** where James talks about innocent suffering brings **Isaiah 53** to mind. But in the case of Jesus it was not only an innocent man suffering at the hands of the rich and powerful, but His innocent suffering for us, which we would remember.

The Lord Hears

1. James' fierce condemnation of the rich in **5:1–6** also contains a plea that they repent before the final judgment occurs. **5:1** may be understood in two ways. On the one hand, James may be saying: "Start to weep and mourn now already because when the Judgment Day comes, you will really weep and mourn." On the other hand, he may also be saying: "Come now, weep with the weeping and mourning of repentance, so that you may be delivered from the judgment upon you for your sinfulness." Both mean-

ings are possible. In either case, the words of James are pointed. They remind us of the parables of the Kingdom **(Matthew 13)**.

2. The concept and the characteristics of the Kingdom will be treated more extensively in the next lesson. Other passages are **Is. 61:1–2; Luke 4:16–21; Matt. 11:2–5; 25:34–40.**

3. Draw two columns on a chalk board or poster board. In one column list the characteristics of the sinfully rich. In the other column list the characteristics of God's Kingdom and His people. Discuss the difference.

The Word for Us

1–4. End the lesson with positive suggestions for the Kingdom use of wealth. It is not wealth that is condemned but the false trust and the misuse of wealth's power that is judged. How does the redeemed child dedicate all to Christ?

Closing

Pray stanza 3 of "What Is the World to Me" as your closing prayer.

Lesson 12
Living Expectantly (James 5:7–12)

Before the Session

If possible, read the section on the end times in a Bible dictionary. Refer to a good commentary as you study this section of James. Pray that God would bless your preparation.

The Class Session

Begin with prayer. Before beginning the session, sit facing the class, stare, and say nothing. The class will probably get quiet and sit and wait. Be silent for as long as you can stand it. Then break the silence and ask how it felt to wait. Were some uncomfortable? How did they show it? Why is it so hard to wait? How is the Christian life a life of waiting? What are we waiting for? Are we impatient? Conclude by reading the "Theme Verse" from the study guide.

Ask for a volunteer to read the "Goal" and "What's Going On Here?" from the study guide. Then begin your study of Scripture.

Searching the Scriptures

What Is Your Hope?

1. The word "patient" in **5:7** has the sense of confident assurance that despite troubles now the believer can have confidence that God is in control of history and Christ will come again. The phrase "Judgment Day" suggests the Law's final condemnation of the sinner in his unbelief.

For the Christian, however, the Lord's coming **(v. 7)** is positive. The final coming is the culmination of the promises of God in the Old and the New Testament. The Old Testament points to Christ. The Gospel points to the future when Christ, who redeemed us, will come again to lead us into the fullness of the salvation He won for us. (See **Rev. 5:1–14; 7:9–17; 19:1–10.**) That anticipated fulfillment permits us to live in joyful expectation. Consider the betrothed or engaged couple who have the promise of life together, yet live expectantly and joyfully in anticipation of the consummation. Our hope gives us a future expectation and also a positive attitude toward the present, so James says in **verse 7**: "Be patient, then, brothers, until the Lord's coming" and in **verse 8**: "You too be patient and stand firm, because the Lord's coming is near."

Patience is a gift of grace—a fruit of faith in Christ. James' encouragement to "be patient" means to live trustingly by faith in Jesus Christ. Trusting in Christ, we expect to receive or experience that for which we ask Him. To trust is to expect. A Christian then lives expectantly while he waits for his trust in Christ to be fulfilled.

When we are tempted to lose hope and become impatient, we are being tempted to forget God, and act as if we had not been forgiven and promised eternal life—as if there were no future in God's promise. By the Gospel of Christ, the Holy Spirit leads us to know our sins are forgiven. The burden of guilt, punishment, and eternal death are behind us (buried in the grave with Christ; see **Rom. 6:3–4**). A new life, hope, and a future to be unfolded lie before us.

2–4. Words and phrases that refer directly to the final coming of the Lord in **chapter 5** are "misery that is coming" **(v. 1)**; "gold and silver," "last days" **(v. 3)**; "cries … have reached the ears of the Lord" **(v. 4)**; "Lord's coming" **(v. 7)**; "an example of patience … the prophets" **(v. 10)**; "prayer offered in faith," "raise him up," "he will be forgiven" **(v. 15)**; "confess," "healed" **(v. 16)**; "prayer of a righteous man" **(v. 16).**

It is evident which words and phrases suggest punishment (the Law). Others express hope and promise (the Gospel).

5. James reminds his readers that the Lord's coming is a sure thing. They are to be patient and not give in to vindictiveness or getting even with

those who oppress them. God is Judge; they are not. The power to exercise this patience is available from the Holy Spirit, for one of His fruits is patience or long suffering **(Gal. 5:22)**.

A Future with Meaning

1. The image of the farmer sowing the seed expectantly is a good illustration of the trust, expectation, and patience with which a Christian can face the future. The phrase "the word planted in you" **(1:21)** may come to mind here, or the words in **3:18** about the "harvest of righteousness" that comes to those who "sow in peace." (Note how certain images recur throughout the epistle, e.g., planting, seed, harvest, birth, etc.)

2–3. To "stand firm" is to be like the man who is blessed when he "perseveres under trial, because when he has stood the test, he will receive the crown of life that God has promised to those who love Him" **(1:12;** also **3:18)**. Related passages for further discussion are **Rom. 13:11–12; Heb. 10: 19–25; 1 Peter 4:7–11**. Only through faith strengthened by the Holy Spirit working through God's Word are we enabled and empowered to stand firm.

The Yes of Faith

1. The phrases "the Lord's coming is near" and "at the door" are encouragements always to live expectantly (see **Matt. 25:13)**. Just as the leaves of the fig tree are signs that summer is coming **(Mark 13:28–30)**, so the signs of the end time, which occur to every generation, are reminders that the event can come at any time.

2. "Sigh," "groan," "grieve" are other meanings for the word translated "grumble." In **4:11–12,** James points out that in speaking evil against a brother a person judges the Law, and that there is only one Lawgiver and Judge. In **5:9,** James says that the Judge is now at the door. Certainly, it is no time to speak evil against others, or even to groan and grumble because others may speak evil against us. Our attention is to be on God's deliverance **(4:12)**. The faithful will live their faith by not speaking evil **(4:11)** and groaning **(5:9),** but in being doers of the Word **(1:22, 27)**. They will be patient **(5:7)** and stand firm **(5:8)**.

3–4. James' phrase "Job's perseverance" **(5:11)** takes us back to the beginning of his epistle. Along with Abraham and Rahab, Job is a classic example of an individual whose steadfast faith and trust in God was "mature and complete, not lacking anything" **(1:4)**. It is important for us to realize that Job, Abraham, Rahab, Elijah **(5:17)** and those mentioned in **Hebrews 11** are not idealized examples "who never had it as rough as we do." Actually, the Scripture accounts describe the intense difficulty and the real struggles of faith that each of these went through.

5. In your discussion of swearing (calling God to witness the truth of our words; different from cursing—asking God to condemn or destroy) emphasize the strength implied in speaking without swearing and our need to renew our faith and confidence so that we can speak simply and truthfully.

The Word for Us

1–4. Patience is a gift—and to be content and patient is very difficult for some. Make this a time to share your difficulty with patience and allow the class to gain insight and strength as they look at their own impatience and weakness of faith. Encourage repentance and renewal in Christ.

Closing

Ask for prayer requests and incorporate them into a closing prayer. Conclude by speaking or singing stanzas 1 and 3 of "Jesus, Still Lead On."

Lesson 13
Personal Care—God's Care (James 5:13–20)

Before the Session

Read through the study guide and leaders notes materials in conjunction with **James 5:13–20.** Consult a Bible commentary, if possible. Remember the participants in prayer and ask the Lord to bless this concluding session so that by the power of His Spirit participants will incorporate the truths they have learned from this study of James into their lives.

Before the Session

Ask a volunteer to begin the session with prayer. Have another person read the "Theme Verse," "Goal," and "What's Going On Here?" from the study guide.

Me, a "Minister"?

1–2. The "ministerial" dimension is basic to every aspect of Christian life together. The function of the church includes care and concern for all people. The phrase "priesthood of believers" emphasizes the ministry common to all Christians. James' focus on brotherhood, the fruits of faith, impartial justice, doing the Word, and humble faith in God are all visible in the care of Christians one for another. See also **5:4, 15–16** as examples of ministry.

Up and At It

1. The distinctive character of Christians in their ministry one to another is service rather than contention. It is being steadfast in the faith and merciful, rather than judgmental and partial. Through faith in Christ, a Christian can be patient, yielding, wise, compassionate **(5:10–11)**; rather than wavering or double-minded **(1:6–8)** or arrogant, hurried, and secretive, legalistic, judgmental, or like the rich taking advantage of the poor. It actually takes faith in Christ to be outgoing rather than selfish. It takes faith to be patient and personal rather than proud and judgmental.

2–3. When discussing the difficulty we have in maintaining our faith in the midst of good and bad times, emphasize the help that God makes readily available to us through Word and Sacraments. Review some of the warnings listed and some of the encouragements to faith life. In every struggle of faith we come to the crucified and risen Christ as our assurance of God's love and His patient reaching to us with His forgiveness.

For the Sick in Body or Spirit

1–2. "Prayer" as a petition is a believer's trusting response to God's invitation to ask Him for help. "Prayer," as distinct from Word and Sacrament, is not a means of grace. Prayer is not a gimmick or technique that a person uses in order to reach God or to change Him. Prayer as a petition (as distinct from prayer as praise and thanksgiving) is a Christian's trusting (or faith) response to God and, therefore, a request for help for self or others.

3. Though the oil might have aided healing, the anointing which James speaks about **(5:14)** is generally considered to be more devotional and symbolical than medicinal. The emphasis is on the "name of the Lord" **(v. 14)** and the "prayer offered in faith" **(v. 15)** to God.

4. **Verse 15** is a statement of promise. The Lord promises to save a person from his illness according to His will. The Lord will raise him up, and He will forgive him his sins. (Related passages are **Matt. 7:7–8; 9:22; Mark 5:23–24; 11:24; John 14:13; 15:7.**)

Prayer

1. Christians praying for one another carry out ministry. James' concluding words contain God's own invitation to us to pray and His promise to hear **(5:16)**.

2. Besides Elijah **(v. 17)** and Abraham **(Gen. 18:22–33)**, the prayer of Daniel **(Dan. 9:17–19)** and of Paul in prison **(Acts 16:25)** are also examples of expectant prayer. Elijah was a man of faith; he also had his difficulties (e.g., **1 Kings 19:2–3**) and weaknesses **(1 Kings 19:9–10)**. But he

trusted in the Lord, and did according to His Word.

3. We who have been made righteous by Christ's death on the cross for our sins always have access to God in prayer. Numerous passages in Scripture indicate that God wants us to pray to Him and promises to hear us. In **Ps. 50:15,** for instance, He tells us to call upon Him in the day of trouble. **Ps. 145:13, 18** assures us that He is "faithful to all His promises and loving toward all He has made. … The Lord is near to all who call on Him." And in **Romans** we read that He "richly blesses all who call on Him" **(10:12).** When God does not seem to answer our prayers in the way we want, we can trust that He has heard them and that He is answering them according to His will and timetable and in a way that is best for us.

4. In our efforts to bring back the wanderer and the sinner, we need a loving attitude. The purpose is not to condemn the erring but to win them. The primary question is, "What does this child of God need to hear to return to his Savior?" A lot of listening will be needed, along with patience and prayer. Discuss ways you might bring back the "inactive" members of your congregation. Those who are secure in their sin need to hear God's Law. Those troubled by their sin need to hear God's Gospel.

The Word for Us

1–4. As you end your study, reemphasize the way in which the book of James should be used. It is not meant to be only a condemnation to instill guilt nor to set up standards of goodness we will never attain. As all of the Law, James shows us our continuing need for a Savior. We are not yet perfect, we have not "attained," and we never will! He is our perfection.

5. Try to come up with specific ways the encouragement to growth in **James** and the powerful call to repentance can be used in individual lives and in your congregation.

Closing

Conclude this study with prayer, asking the Lord to help participants apply in word and deed the insights they have discovered from their study of **James.** Then sing or speak stanzas 1, 2, and 6 of "Come, My Soul, with Every Care."

Find Healing in . . .

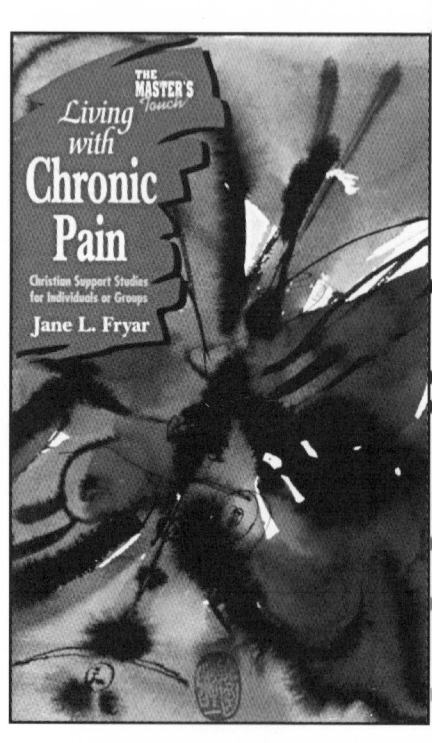

*J*esus' healing touch of love, hope and forgiveness will help you find positive solutions to the concerns weighing on your heart. As you study and share His Word, the Holy Sprit will lead you to grow in spiritual maturity and deeper faith experiences, and even reach out to those who face similar needs and concerns.

Four to five sessions each . . .

*Living with **Chronic Pain***
*Suffering from **Guilt***
*Living with **Change***
*Coping with **Compassion Fatigue***
*Living with **Compulsive Behaviors***
*Discovering **Life after Divorce***
*Living with **Infertility***
*Surviving **Sexual Abuse***
*Living with **Too Little Time***
*Coping with **Stress***
*Living with **Grief***

*Living with **Terminal Illness***
***AIDS:** A Christian Perspective*
*Living with **Workaholism***
*Surviving **Financial Crisis***
*Overcoming **Depression***

Concordia
Publishing House

www.cph.org